LISA NANDY

ALL IN

HOW WE BUILD A COUNTRY THAT WORKS

HarperNorth

HarperNorth
Windmill Green
24 Mount Street
Manchester, M2 3NX

A division of
HarperCollins*Publishers*
1 London Bridge Street
London SE1 9GF

www.harpercollins.co.uk

HarperCollins*Publishers*
Macken House, 39/40 Mayor Street Upper
Dublin 1, D01 C9W8, Ireland

First published by HarperNorth in 2022
This revised and updated edition published 2023

1 3 5 7 9 10 8 6 4 2

A catalogue record for this book
is available from the British Library

PB ISBN: 978-0-00-848080-6

Printed and bound in the UK using 100%
renewable electricity at CPI Group (UK) Ltd

For Otis

CONTENTS

BRITAIN ISN'T WORKING

'We choose to go to the moon in this decade not
because it is easy but because it is hard.'

John F. Kennedy

For the last thirteen years I have represented a town buffeted
by waves of political upheaval, global crises and economic
failures that have left Britain reeling. During that time, I have
served as the UK's Shadow Foreign Secretary, which offered
a window onto the global failures that have shaped Britain's
current crisis, and I have been Shadow Secretary of State for
Levelling Up, Housing and Communities, giving me a front-
row seat on the challenges people are experiencing in their
everyday lives as the cost-of-living crisis bites.

I have grappled with the challenges experienced at local
and national level. I have learnt from some of the most excit-
ing, radical, creative people in Britain and across the world.
And I have watched as one by one they have been defeated
by a status quo that tilts power and resources away from
people with a stake in the outcome – the builders, makers
and creators.

Britain can't go on like this – we all know it. Even before
the pandemic, war in Ukraine, soaring inflation and the

disastrous Truss Government which sent the economy into freefall, voters were sounding the alarm on a political and economic settlement that wasn't delivering. They have shown me, through their everyday pragmatism and quiet patriotism, how Britain can and must adapt to a new era.

As the era of globalisation gives way to an era of resilience, our politics has struggled to catch up. Discontent is bubbling up from below, from the people and places who lost in the last chapter of our national story. It is also driven from above: the seismic upheaval of geopolitics has created an irresistible logic for greater security, certainty, national and local resilience. Responding to this transition is the challenge of our age.

In 1945 the Attlee Government rose to the post-war moment with a programme of national renewal, bringing common goods into common ownership and building public housing on a scale never seen before. In the 1960s and 1970s the Wilson Government responded to the women, immigrants and working-class families whose ambition outstripped the opportunities on offer with the Equal Pay Act, Race Relations Act and comprehensive education. In the 1990s the Blair Government responded to globalisation with the mantra 'Education, education, education', investing in early years centres, rebuilding crumbling schools and expanding higher education to try to ensure Britain's young people could compete in the world.

Now, tasked by the Labour Party with answering the question of how to work our way out of our current crisis, I am determined that we seize this moment and rise to meet the challenge of our age: to build a country in which everyone has a stake and a contribution to make. In short, to rebuild Britain the only way we can – together.

It is a journey that has taken me across Britain and around the world. It has led me to reimagine the role of government, think anew about the role of markets and draw on Britain's natural assets. Greatest amongst these assets are the contributions of those parts of our country that within living memory powered the world and the quiet patriotism at work in every region and nation that is creating the radical change we need.

While we are still shackled by a remote, centralised system of governance, built for a different age, now is the time to remember that we achieve more by our common endeavour than we achieve alone. Only by being 'all in' can we match people's ambition and make Britain work again.

With politics in crisis, the economy broken and hope in short supply, this is the time to start afresh and build the country I've believed in all my life but never yet quite seen. This book is about how.

1.

THE CHALLENGE

I can still remember the moment. I was looking out towards the East stand at the DW Stadium as Wigan Athletic played. The ball hit the back of the net. A roar of noise engulfed us.

A friend leaned over and said, 'It must be a big feeling.' She didn't mean the score. She was reminding me that many of those people cheering on the Latics, the majority perfect strangers, had put their cross on a ballot paper next to my name only a couple of weeks earlier.

It is awesome, in a literal sense, to be elected – to be tasked with decisions that have the potential to shape and define people's lives, community and country. What I didn't know then is that over the next decade those people would come to shape and define me and the things I believe in.

They are the people who have built and sustained everything of value in our community: the grassroots football, rugby league and labour clubs, and the credit unions and community centres that have seen us through good times and bad. But too often they are thwarted by a system in which other people hold all the cards.

My town, Wigan, is famous the world over for the way we pull together in tough times, whether in the battle we fought to save the coal mines from closure in the 1980s or the grit, struggle and kindness of the depression years made famous by George Orwell in *The Road to Wigan Pier*. But, like so many others in Britain and around the world, we have been battling a system that at best fails to protect the things that matter to us, and at worst has completely undermined them.

I saw this for myself in 2019 when Bury Football Club went into administration and, agonisingly, after being bought and sold by a chain of rotten owners, was expelled from the Football League. Bury is a Lancashire town, near to Wigan, where I spent my teenage years. My stepdad was a lifelong attendee at Gigg Lane. His final words to my stepbrother when he died in a Lancashire hospice a few years ago were 'What's the score?' Bury fans, known as Shakers, fought a spirited campaign with the help of their local MP, James Frith, but to no avail. After its collapse those fans would gather at Gigg Lane on Saturdays unsure of where to be without the familiar drumbeat of a ritual and tradition that had belonged to them, their families and their community for over a century.

Two years later, I felt history repeating itself. I was standing on College Green outside Parliament, just a few weeks into the job as Labour's Shadow Foreign Secretary, when I took a phone call that would change the way I think about the world and our place in it.

The Chief Executive of Wigan Athletic, Jonathan Jackson, was calling to tell me that our 89-year-strong football club – well-run, much loved, with no significant debts and part of the social fabric of our town – had been plunged into administration.

It didn't make sense.

A new owner, based in Hong Kong, had been approved by the English Football League just days before. He had paid, it turned out, a whopping £41 million for the club, called an immediate board meeting, and put it straight into administration.

In many ways Wigan Athletic personifies the traditional football club. It is anchored in the community – walk into any local school and you'll find coaches or players helping the kids to dream big and plan better – and for so many years it was owned by a local benefactor, whose tenure took us all the way to Wembley, defeating Man City to seize the FA Cup. It was the stuff of legend. So for fans in Wigan it felt like the bottom was falling out of their world.

For the next nine months, from the day of that phone call, we battled to save the club. Those months trying to save Wigan Athletic inspired me to write this book. It taught me to look harder at the cause of the problems so many people have to endure in Britain – the lack of good jobs, low wages and insecure work; declining high streets; frequent flooding; and of course, COVID-19. I came to see that these are problems which are felt locally but can only be solved globally, driven by active national governments taking their cues from people in places like Wigan. I am convinced that if we understand those cues and have the will to respond, we can work with like-minded governments across the world to deliver the change they need. After all, my party, Labour, has always been strongly internationalist.

But as our football club fell apart, it became apparent that if change was coming, it would come only from ourselves. Administrators were brought in and set about selling off the assets. We watched as players who had been the heart and soul of the club were traded away at knockdown prices. The administrators charged hundreds of pounds an hour while staff who had worked for the club for years were laid off. I stood on the sidelines of the first press conference watching a performance play out for the assembled national media while staff I had grown to like and admire over many years stood in tears at the back of the room. The administrators sold players, buildings, equipment. They even sold the washing machines.

Potential buyers surfaced, dozens and dozens of them from across the world. I spent countless hours on the phone listening to total time wasters who said they wanted to buy the club but turned out to have no money, just a desire to play at being football owners. Others were hugely wealthy but showed only a passing interest, disappearing when it became clear this was a long-term investment, not a chance to make a quick buck. During those months I came across some of the most dubious people I have ever met in my life. I learnt how football is home to criminal gangs and networks who buy clubs to hide their assets, launder their money and their reputations and to ensure their owners exist in a privileged sphere, beyond the reach of the UK Government and the rules and the laws that apply to the rest of us.

We set up mental health groups for fans, and the club's senior managers did all they could to protect staff. The Chief Executive continued to work unpaid day and night to save the club. The manager personally rang every single staff member who had been laid off – the caterers, receptionists and groundsmen who had been part of the Wigan Athletic family and were reeling from the news. It meant the world to them. And we watched as all the systems that were set up to protect a club which had stood at the centre of our town for nearly a century fell one by one. Fans and a community that should have been at the heart of the process were shut out, treated as a nuisance by wealthy and powerful people with no connection to the club, not just in the UK but across the world. When it came to the crunch, the wrong people held all the power.

The true story of what had happened to Wigan Athletic may never be known. One leading football journalist called it 'one of the most unlikely and baffling scenarios ever thrown up even among the frequently outlandish sagas of football's relationship with money'.[1] Rumours swirled that the first Hong Kong owner had sold it to another to hide a gambling debt and I searched high and low for answers. It was a journey that took me into a world I had never set foot in before, to the highest levels of the English Football League, into the world of global football gambling and all the way to the Hong Kong Stock Exchange. The suggestions about the Hong Kong takeover were never proven. But for so many of us, the story was already clear and it was far too familiar – of a system that allows the things that matter most to people to be sold off as playthings and get-rich-quick schemes for the wealthy and powerful. When help was sought, from government ministers, or from the institutions that were meant to protect us, with only a handful of exceptions we found them to be hopeless, helpless or, worst of all – on the wrong side.

So we fought back, and in doing so we told a different story about how things could be. We had help from clubs across the country, including amazing support from the Bury campaigners. Those who had tried valiantly to save their own clubs, and sometimes succeeded, gave us hours of their time. The chair of our local supporters' trust worked late into the night, every night, to save the club, while by day she was running a busy secondary school keeping children learning during an unprecedented global pandemic. We launched a 'Plan B' fundraising appeal to buy the club if no owners could be found and raised £615,000 in under a week. This in a town with one of the highest proportions of low earners in Britain. I will never forget the elderly man who walked into the DW Stadium reception with an envelope in his hand containing his entire life savings – a few hundred pounds. It was everything he had, and he needed the club to have it.

These are the incredible people who saved our club. We were helped by some rare and brilliant individuals in the establishment – whether national journalists or top officials – who knew what they were seeing was wrong, who leaked us information and did us no end of favours. They picked up the phone to me on evenings and weekends and helped us defend our club from the sharks that were circling. And while we were failed by the national and international systems that should have protected us, we were lifted by our local institutions. Local athletes and former players like Emmerson Boyce and Jenny Meadows came onto podcast after podcast, raised money and kept the flame of hope alive. Our local newspaper, the *Wigan Evening Post*, battled misinformation, refusing to publish rumours that would put our plans in jeopardy and dialled up the pressure when the greed of those involved stalled the process and threatened to sink us for good. Our local council were quick to intervene, invoking a clause in the deeds to the stadium that they'd written into the contract years before, which allowed them to stop the stadium from being used for anything other than football or rugby league. Without them, as the vultures circled, we would have lost the lot.

Jonathan Jackson, by then one of the many casualties of administration, did more than anybody else. He gave his heart and soul to steer the club through the most turbulent period in its existence. And, finally, he called to confirm that the sale of the club to new owners, whose intentions we had good reason to believe were sincere, had gone through. The club was saved, and after nine agonising, exhausting months we were able to share the news with the town and the world.

This is not just a story about how localism won out and saved the day. If anything, the struggle to save Wigan Athletic shows how much national and international systems matter. Ask any one of the hundreds of people who lost their jobs, or the fans who joined the mental health support groups, and they will tell you those systems should have been there for us – not on the side of the wealthy and powerful at their expense. And they will tell you that when they fail, the local consequences are appalling.

My politics is driven by the experiences of people in places like Wigan. But the treatment of Wigan Athletic exposes the limitations of the idea that local action alone can be a substitute for active, empowering national governments who are prepared to go out and fight for a global system that defends people before profit. The slogans that have become fashionable amongst politicians on left and right – that a rotten Westminster system has outlived its usefulness, or that we can take back control by cutting ourselves off from the world – offer no future to a club like Wigan Athletic or a town like Wigan. They are political devices designed to divert attention from the lack of will, imagination or intellect needed to fix a global and national system that is broken.

I felt it in a café in Halifax, when I watched the owner burst into tears as she described the second set of floods that had devastated her business in three years. She didn't mention COP26, the global summit on climate change that Britain would shortly go on to host. And no wonder: COP is a closed event where leaders thrash out deals behind closed doors. But for her and her family, everything was riding on its success. Just months later at that summit, political leaders failed to agree a pathway to limit global warming to 1.5 degrees.

I heard it in my constituency surgery listening to an elderly man describe in disbelief how he'd been cheated out of his life savings by one of the growing numbers of organised crime gangs whose tentacles stretch across the globe. The power of those criminal gangs is unmatched by the under-resourced, fragmented national crime-fighting agencies who have too few tools at their disposal – and the problems run deeper than this.

In towns and cities across the country people have lived out the reality of global and national failures. So often, it is true that the local response to such failure can be, and has been, magnificent, but the odds are stacked against us.

We now face a crisis where millions of people have watched the foundations of a decent secure life fall apart. And it is a failure to act that has led us here. Decades ago, the uncritical embrace of economic globalisation ushered in an era where people in towns like Wigan were no longer seen as contributors, but as part of the problem itself. Their wages were too high, their demands for protections too many, so their work was transferred to countries where this 'problem' was removed.

Wigan, like many towns, has lived through a long period of industrial decline, forcing young people to look elsewhere for a future and leaving older people to grow old hundreds of miles from their children and grandchildren. All the things I see in my constituency inbox – the crisis of loneliness, crumbling high streets, community pub closures and cancelled bus networks – connect back to that loss of skilled, secure work that has cost us working-age population and spending power.

These are problems felt locally but caused by a global consensus whose roots stretch back to 1979, the year I was born and whose effects are now playing out across Britain, the United States and Europe.

These are the failures, whether by intention or inaction, that have led us to a place where people no longer feel they have a stake in the system, driving the seismic political earthquakes of recent years. It was no accident that the two great upheavals of recent years – Brexit in the United Kingdom, and the election of Donald Trump in the United States – were largely driven by people in towns that had fallen victim to this global pact. Slogans like 'Take Back Control' and 'Make America Great Again' spoke directly to people who wanted a renewed stake in the system. Systems imposed on people from afar, without their consent or inclusion, in the end always fail.

Looked at like this, the rise of strong-man populist leaders who weaponise this anger, demonise minorities and shake our faith in one another and in the system are symptoms of a system that is broken and offer clues as to how it might be fixed. And while democracy provides the only alternative, we have neither served it well nor defended it enough.

But it is my firm belief that the anger which is evident in so many parts of the country and the rejection of the status quo come not from a pessimistic view of the future, but an optimism and ambition for family, community and country that is presently unmatched by our politicians. We should have learnt in recent years that the desire for agency and control, and the demand for a stake in the system, is a major political force that could propel us towards a better future. I am convinced that the anger of recent years springs from the certain knowledge that the future could and should be better. The public see it and for so long they've tried to give voice to it. They are smarter than we are and this book is for them.

2.

THE WORLD TRANSFORMED

'The old order changeth, yielding place to new.'

Alfred, Lord Tennyson

'Freedom' was the word that echoed around the room. I was listening to young people involved in the Arab Spring uprisings who had gathered at a secret location in Tunisia. That word – freedom – was never far from their lips or their thoughts. Through them, the struggle for the future was playing out.

I was in Tunisia for a conference dominated by older, male leaders of the Arab countries whose young people were finding their voice on the streets and meeting halls just a few miles – but an entire world away – from that staid, air-conditioned hotel.

Those brave young people were in a struggle for power with those who had always held it and wouldn't relinquish it easily. But they could not be denied it. I listened to a teenage girl whose family had disowned her for getting involved in politics and a young man whose friends had been killed in a protest. It was less the hope that freedom would come that kept them going, more the certain knowledge of what life was like without it.

This was a clash of the generations. The world's population has roughly tripled since 1945 and it has been uneven, creating mirror-image challenges – ageing populations in countries like ours and younger populations in countries like theirs. It has gifted us a generation of young people with hopes and expectations for change that are unmatched by the world we have created.

Those young people had reasons to be hopeful. Most of them were among the beneficiaries of one of the great success stories of the last forty years: the huge expansion of global education that has touched millions who were shut out before, especially young women. Since 1979 the number of girls who are unable to go to school has halved to just over 3 per cent of all 0–15s as the global population has increased by 60 per cent.[1]

Not a single one of them took it for granted. The same was true of the young people of Afghanistan who I Zoomed regularly with during the summer of 2021, who had complex feelings about Britain's involvement in their country over twenty years, a country they yearned to govern for themselves. But as the Taliban advanced, there was nothing complicated in their minds about the life-changing educational opportunities that had opened up to them and the promise of a life that allowed them to contribute to their country and the world, rapidly disappearing in front of their eyes.

They are right to expect more. In 1979 there were so few women parliamentarians globally that the Inter-Parliamentary Union didn't even bother to count them. By 1997 one in ten legislators were women. Since then, that has doubled to one in five.[2]

Advances in education, science and technology have, as the forward-thinking scientist James Burke predicted as far back as 1985, offered us the prospect of putting a rocket under this advancement, should we choose to. On a television programme entitled 'Worlds Without End' he painted a vision of the plural, open, democratic future we could create:

'With it we could operate on the basis that ethics and standards and values and facts and truth all depend on what your view of the world is and that there may be as many views of that as there are people. And with this [technology] capable of keeping a tally on the millions of opinions voiced electronically, we might be able to list the limitations of conforming to any centralised representational form of government originally invented because there was no way for everybody's voice to be heard.

'You might be able to give everybody unhindered, untested access to knowledge because a computer would do the day-to-day work for which we once qualified the select few in an educational system designed for a world in which only the few could be taught. You might end the regimentation of people working in vast unmanageable cities, uniting them instead in an electronic community where the Himalayas and Manhattan were only a split second apart.

'You might with that and much more break the mould that has held us back since the beginning in a future world that we would describe as balanced anarchy and they will describe as an open society, tolerant of every view and where there is no single privileged way of doing things. Above all, able to do away with the greatest tragedy of our era. The centuries old waste of human talent that we wouldn't or couldn't use. Utopia? Why? If as I've said all along the universe is at any time what you say it is, then say.'

This was the future the young people of the Arab Spring described to me that day in Tunisia. This was their moment to seize those opportunities and shape the universe. Democracy was the prize, but we had neither served it well nor defended it enough to help those young people create the future they had glimpsed.

The march of global progress that once seemed inevitable has halted. For all the advances, women remain shut out from wealth and power. Men own 50 per cent more of the world's wealth than women, women are paid half male salaries and still, even now, there are only a handful of women leaders around the world.[3] After fifteen consecutive years in which freedom has been in retreat – with the rights of individuals under attack, often from their own governments – 2019 became the first year that income from autocratic regimes outstripped that of democracies. The *Economist* estimates that the autocratic world accounts for over 30 per cent of global GDP, and its share of global exports has soared from just 3 per cent in 1989 to 30 per cent today. A third of the goods imported by democracies come from non-democratic countries. The global economy is integrated in a way that it never was before.[4]

The great leveller that James Burke described was now a reality, and for the young people I met in Tunisia that day, theirs was a revolution made possible by new technology. But it was also a revolution crushed by the ownership and concentration of that technology in a few hands. Within months the revolution was over, crushed in almost every country across the Middle East, and with it the hopes of a generation. The forward march of freedom was halted.

Those young people told a story about the way the world has changed, for better and worse, which we often miss in our myopic political debate. The world we live in now is younger, more educated, but less free than it was in 1979. We are richer than we were, but less equal and less happy. We are more interconnected but far more divided.

So much of the last forty years should give us, and them, cause for hope but it has thrown up new challenges that call forward a new generation to respond, unencumbered by the dogmas of the past. Encapsulated in the story of those young people and so much that drove the eventual defeat of their democratic uprising is our failure to respond to the way the world has changed – and we must.

THE END OF CERTAINTY

In 1989 the Berlin Wall fell and with it the certainties of the Cold War era. It set in train a series of events which, as the historian Eric Hobsbawm argued, brought to an end the twentieth century – a century characterised by the end of European dominance, war, atrocity and the search for peace, and extraordinary progress in science and technology.[5]

That century belonged to the United States. A nation of 4 million citizens when it was founded in 1789 had, by 1989, become a nation of 250 million. It was a period of growth in wealth and personal freedom unequalled in history, matched by the growing power and influence of the United States across the world. According to one of its greatest chroniclers and champions, the legendary *Times* editor Harry Evans: 'In the twentieth century the essentially isolationist American people did more than grow rich and expand their domestic freedoms. They sustained Western Civilization by acts of courage, generosity and vision unparalleled in the history of man. They concerted the defeat of the Fascist tyranny and they contained Soviet totalitarianism until it buried itself.'[6]

This characterisation of the United States as a standard bearer for freedom was of course rightly contested by those who pointed to the smallness of American democracy itself, the millions denied rights in US-held territories, particularly in Asia, and the impact of the USA in many countries around the world during the Cold War years, not least Vietnam. But the choice made by Harry Truman to come to Europe's aid – and underwrite its economic and military security – was significant, sparking an era in which successive American presidents accepted a self-declared role as the 'leader of the free world'.

Did they succeed? Not always, perhaps not often. As Danny Finkelstein puts it, 'sometimes they lost their way, sometimes they were too strong, sometimes too weak, but always they accepted the American post-war duty, a self-imposed duty, to show a way forward, to rally liberal democracies, to support the opinion and actions of the free nations'.[7] While many resisted American hegemony, that it existed was never seriously in doubt.

That era ended with a bang with the election of Donald Trump, whose promise to Make America Great Again spoke to an American people who had grown weary of acting as the world's policeman while jobs disappeared and living standards crumbled. But in truth, decades before the 2016 Presidential Election the hegemonic twentieth century was already giving way to a multipolar world.

Global power shifted as the population in developing countries swelled. Africa is now growing so rapidly that by 2050 there will be more people in Nigeria than the United States. The global map is changing before our eyes. An ageing Europe is shrinking as Asia – now home to 60 per cent of the world's population – expands. There are almost 1.5 billion people in China alone.

Economic gravity has shifted eastwards. The rise of China is by far the most remarkable aspect of recent decades. In 1979 the Chinese Communist Government opened up the Chinese economy to foreign trade and investment, making

China one of the fastest-growing economies in the world. It was described by the World Bank as 'the fastest sustained expansion by a major economy in history'.[8] China's was the only economy to grow in 2020, in the middle of the global pandemic. In 1995 the UK's economy was twice as big as China's. Today China's economy is roughly five times the size of the UK. By 2028 China will outstrip the economic power of the USA, with Brazil and India snapping at its heels.

This is a country whose economic reach now extends across the globe. It is also a totalitarian state that commits genocide against the Uyghur Muslims in Xinjiang, has dismantled democratic freedoms in Hong Kong, frequently displays aggression towards Taiwan, and has used its Belt and Road Initiative – providing low-cost finance to developing countries – to extend not just its economic reach but its political power, seizing major assets in countries where repayments are impossible, and subverting democracy in the process. Though China has gone 'to some lengths to say that its big idea is non-prescriptive, consensus-based and aimed at creating a multi-polar world structure, one where the old dominance of a single power alone is consigned to history'[9] under Xi Jinping it has projected power beyond its borders, portraying itself at times as the centre of a new world order. It may well yet succeed in creating that new world order, but unlike the previous settlement the world it leads is not one that will be rooted in individual liberty. A leader of the free world no longer exists.

The world, and the values that underpin it, are spinning on its axis. For my grandfather, who earned the Légion d'Honneur for his role in the liberation of Paris and later entered Parliament as a Liberal MP, theirs was a straightforward fight for freedom, a clash between repressive communist states and open capitalist democracies, between liberal democracy and authoritarianism. What would his generation have made of the unique and unprecedented challenge posed by the blend of authoritarian capitalism pursued by China since 1979?

We grew used to thinking of the world 'in terms of binary opposites, capitalism and socialism, as alternatives mutually excluding each other', wrote another of his generation, Eric Hobsbawm, in 1994. 'It should now be becoming clear that this was an arbitrary and to some extent artificial construction, which can only be understood as part of a particular historical context.'[10]

It falls to our generation to respond, but we are divided amongst ourselves as to how to respond. Some advocate conflict with China, others containment. Some seek competition, others cooperation. But as Kerry Brown puts it, 'it is no longer a question of containing China. China contains us.'[11] And China is but the biggest, most pressing and most challenging example of authoritarian states – Russia, Saudi Arabia, Iran – that must often be challenged, but can be neither defeated nor isolated, without risking appalling consequences. Whether it's the rapid advance of new diseases or drones that can be deployed at the touch of a button, the cyber-attacks that can bring financial systems to their knees, or the race to own space and the satellite technology that affects lives around the globe, the world beyond our shores, and those who govern it, cannot be ignored. With the end of Pax Americana and the rise of China, Russia and other authoritarian regimes, the world has to find new ways to cooperate. But can we?

In this new complex reality, the institutions that reflect the post-World War II order look increasingly anachronistic and outdated. Designed in a different age, they have proven to be – as Abraham Lincoln once said – 'inadequate to the stormy present'.

Take the United Nations, a beacon of hope for so many, founded on the most radical and essential of ideas, that security and progress is only possible through dialogue, especially with those with whom you disagree. It was created, as the former Secretary General Dag Hammarskjold tells it, not 'to take mankind to heaven but to save humanity from hell'.[12] When it was founded, the UN had fifty-one member states. Today, as European empires and the USSR have crumbled into the dust, its 193 member states are unable to reach global agreement on so many of our collective challenges. The power of authoritarian states has meant that progress on major conflicts, like Syria, a war that has raged longer than World Wars I and II combined, has run into the sand. Meanwhile, existential challenges like climate change have been parked in a box marked 'too difficult'.

Meanwhile the European Union, founded in the wake of World War II to build the close economic ties that, in the words of one of its founding fathers Robert Schuman, would make war in Europe 'not merely unthinkable but materially impossible', has become strained in recent years with the departure of Britain, the dependence of many EU countries on Russia for energy, and tensions on open display between richer and poorer member states. During COVID-19, while European countries struggled to agree a package to come to the aid of poorer southern countries, China stepped in, prompting the Serbian president to declare, 'European solidarity does not exist. That was a fairy tale on paper. The only ones who can help ... that is China.'[13]

As the sand shifts beneath our feet, cooperation looks ever more difficult. The pandemic, a stark and immediate reminder that our destinies are bound together, broke the world apart as borders closed, migrants and minorities were scapegoated and Sinophobia spread. A scramble for protective equipment dramatically inflated prices, and vaccine nationalism swept across the world. Populist, nationalist rhetoric from political leaders put institutions that embodied cooperation, like the World Health Organization, directly in the line of fire. There was no greater symbol of the end of the American Century than its withdrawal from the World Health Organization in the middle of a global pandemic.

It has been, said the UN secretary general, António Guterres, like 'an x-ray, revealing fractures in the fragile skeleton of the societies we have built. It is exposing fallacies and falsehoods everywhere: The lie that free markets can deliver healthcare for all; the fiction that unpaid care work is not work; the delusion that we live in a post-racist world; the myth that we are all in the same boat.'[14]

This was a response that flew in the face of all self-interest everywhere. As the virus reached every corner of the globe it was clear that to defeat COVID-19 anywhere it had to be defeated everywhere. The International Monetary Fund called investment in the vaccine 'the biggest return on investment in modern history' but the ongoing failure to cooperate cost lives and livelihoods. 'The biggest challenge we face', said the director general of the World Health Organization, 'is not the virus itself but the lack of solidarity globally and locally.' Even a year after the vaccine was first administered, less than half of the world had been fully vaccinated and new variants continued to cause devastation in rich and poor countries alike.[15]

But while our broken politics had few answers, elsewhere another vision of the future was playing out. Regularly through the pandemic I Zoomed with the scientists – Chinese, American, British, European and many more besides – who were cooperating across borders even as the political environment became more toxic and the personal risks, to them and their families, grew. Between them, in record time, they discovered the treatment, diagnostics and vaccines that have already saved millions of lives. Theirs is the spirit we need to summon for the challenges that lie ahead.

GO FAST, TOGETHER

The greatest and most pressing of these challenges is climate change, an existential question that reminds us in this fragmented and uncertain world that our destinies are bound together like never before. On the road to net zero there is no scope for free riding, and no short cuts. Without action from all of us, everywhere, no place on earth is safe.

In 2021, one of the cooler years on recent record, the aptly named Furnace Creek in Death Valley recorded an incredible, record-breaking temperature of 54 degrees Celsius. In the same month Turkey, Finland and the northern pacific coast of North America registered record heat, while more than 40 per cent of the Greenland ice cap was covered in meltwater. In the last few years wildfires have engulfed parts of Greater Manchester, Lancashire, Yorkshire, Wales and Scotland, ensuring that large swathes of the UK experienced the devastation common to California, the Mediterranean and Australia. July 2022 witnessed Britain's first 40-degree day, and wildfires burned forty homes to the ground in the capital.

If temperatures rise by 3 degrees above industrial levels, the world will be utterly transformed. As ice melts and sea levels and temperatures rise, coastal cities, the Amazon rainforest and coral reefs will likely disappear. This is not just a distant prospect. In Gwynedd in Wales the 450 residents of Fairbourne have already been told that rising sea levels mean their homes will be lost to the sea in the next three decades. The policy of managed retreat has major implications. Land, food and water shortages will create more famine, war and hunger. The Intergovernmental Panel on Climate Change estimates that, at 3 degrees, cereal prices might be as much as 29 per cent higher, putting another 183 million of us at risk of hunger.

As if the threat to life weren't alone enough, climate change looks set to ravage our finances too. In a speech in 2015 the (then) Governor of the Bank of England Mark Carney made headlines when he said climate change was the greatest threat to the world economy. In his speech, 'Breaking the Tragedy of the Horizon',[16] Carney set out how climate change could upend the global economy. Alongside major insurance claims for floods, storms and compensation, he raised the prospect that a rapid revaluation of assets bound up in fossil fuels could leave trillions of assets stranded as the world transitions to a low-carbon economy. With so much of the world's pensions, savings and institutions bound up in investments in fossil fuels, he warned, the failure to divest was the biggest threat to the global financial system and the livelihoods and economic security of millions who depend on it.

That is why leaders like Anthony Albanese in Australia are prioritising action on climate change, to open the door to 'a new era of prosperity' as the fossil fuel jobs that have sustained Australia begin to disappear. He follows the Ardern government in New Zealand, which became the first in the world to rein in the global financial risks created by climate change with tough legislation because it is not only the poorest abroad who suffer from inaction on the climate emergency. Working-class people in New Zealand and in Britain whose pensions and savings are bound up in fossil fuels stand to lose most if we do not act now.

There is a widely quoted saying, 'If you want to go fast go alone, if you want to go far go together.' Today's challenge is to go fast, together. While we are light years away from where we should be, there have been moments in recent history when we have risen to the occasion.

In December 2015 I arrived at the Paris Climate Conference with a sense of trepidation. There were high expectations among political leaders and young activists alike, but the anxiety was palpable. The previous conference, four years earlier in Copenhagen, had fallen apart in the final, early hours of the morning driven by deeply entrenched divisions between the northern and southern hemispheres. Countries who had benefited from growth built on an industrial model that had taken its toll on the planet were asking newly industrialising countries to forgo that same growth model. For so long so many had worked to build bridges across this divide. Was this the moment we would succeed?

Two of the biggest emitting countries, China and the USA, were able to reach agreement before the summit began, allowing President Obama and Chinese Premier Li Keqiang to come together, alongside the host President Hollande of France, to target pledges that would keep global warming well below 1.5 degrees Celsius. Mayors of the world's biggest cities – Paris's Anne Hidalgo, New York's Bill De Blasio and Rio's Eduardo Paes chief among them – stood together to launch ambitious plans to power the lives of millions through clean energy in cities across the world.

But it was a group of women leaders – nicknamed The Lionesses – who are widely credited with the success of the Paris Conference. Headed by the UN's climate chief, Christiana Figueres, once dubbed 'the woman who saved the planet', they included: Laurence Tubiana, the climate ambassador to the French President; Rachel Kyte, the climate advisor to the UN secretary general; and Kate Hampton, a leading actor in the philanthropy movement who heads up the Children's Investment Fund. Theirs was the painstaking work, beginning the day that Copenhagen failed, which led to agreement in Paris. When it was announced, delegates, and the world, breathed a collective sigh of relief.

The Paris Agreement created a compact to target global warming to well below 1.5 degrees Celsius above industrial levels. It allowed countries to decide themselves on how far and fast they could go, reflecting the very different situations of different countries, some far more heavily reliant on fossil fuels – vital given the stakes for working people around the world. Was it enough? No. But it was an agreement struck in the hope and expectation that as technology advanced and new options arose we would move further and faster together.

RISE TOGETHER ... OR FALL APART

Instead, since Paris, the world has seen a continuation of trends that splinter the world apart in the face of our greatest collective challenge. The gulf between richer and poorer countries has continued to grow. Advanced countries are asking developing economies not to use the assets they have to drive economic growth using the same model we did. Poorer countries rich in fossil fuels they could burn or forests they could exploit are understandably seeking compensation for the move towards clean tech. Countries that rely heavily on coal or forestry for energy supply and economic growth – like the US, India, Australia, Brazil and China – lag behind those who don't.

The world continues to heat up, leading to land, food and water shortages. This, in turn, is creating war, conflict and migration flows as people are forced to move. Politicians have capitalised on this, pitting poorer people here against poorer people overseas. In 2020 the anti-fascist group Hope Not

Hate published a stark warning to politicians to take climate change more seriously. Their investigation found that 'while most on the far right are doing everything in their power to question climate change and impede action, a small minority on the violent fringe are adopting a language of eco-fascism to justify their hate-filled agenda and even violence'. This warning turned out to be prescient. In 2022 the UK Government decided to tear up its international and moral obligations to provide sanctuary, sending asylum seekers to Rwanda, not just for processing but, they hoped, for good. In Australia it also fuelled Brexit-style divisions, between younger, middle-class voters in cities who rightly want faster action on climate change and older, working-class voters in towns, whose livelihoods, and the future for their children and their communities, are currently dependent on fossil fuels. Anthony Albanese's Labor Party, elected on a pledge to end the climate wars, offers hope that with political will these divisions can be transcended.

In recent years the stranglehold of Russia over much of Europe's gas supplies has driven not just economic uncertainty but so much of the political chaos that has followed. As Helen Thompson has argued, energy and our political response to it is at the root of much of the political chaos that has been unleashed.[17]

Because it is poorer people everywhere who lose the most. Whether the business owners dealing with flooding in Halifax or the plight of the people of the Republic of Kiribati in the Pacific Ocean, lying six feet above sea level, poorer people in wealthy and poorer nations alike are more exposed and less able to adapt their livelihoods, security, homes and communities, all on the line in the fight against climate change.

A DIFFERENT SORT OF LEADERSHIP

To pull us back from the brink we need a new generation of leaders, guided by clear principles, able to work with those with whom they have profound disagreement, without ever veering off course.

The complexity of the challenge is highlighted by the critical role of China. Without China no action on climate change is possible. Not only does it produce 27 per cent of the world's greenhouse gas emissions – more than the entire developed world combined – but as we transition to renewable energy, and the world becomes less dependent for energy imports on authoritarian countries such as Saudi Arabia and Russia – a process that has belatedly gathered pace since the Russian invasion of Ukraine, exacerbating the crisis in energy, food and living costs across Europe – we become far more dependent on others like China where the raw materials needed for renewables are found.

Half of all the world's polysilicon – a key material in solar panels – comes from the Xinjiang province of China.[18] Xinjiang is also where the Chinese authorities are committing genocide against the Uyghur Muslims – confirmed by both the United Nations and the independent Uyghur Tribunal.[19] Last year, the UK Parliament became one of the first in the world to recognise what was happening to the Uyghur as genocide and sought to limit trade with China. But at the same time, the UK was seeking to convince China that without greater action on climate change the battle for climate safety was bound to fail.

Growing tensions developed between human rights advocates, who argued China must be isolated, and environmental activists, who argued that negotiation on climate could not wait. They are both right. Ignoring human rights is unconscionable. Ignoring climate change is impossible.

But ultimately, efforts on both fronts did not succeed. Although President Xi announced he would phase out investment in overseas coal-fired power stations, he did not even attend the landmark 2021 COP26 summit in Glasgow and calls for more help for developing countries went largely unheeded. The persecution of the Uyghurs continues – thousands of photographs of detainees and a 'shoot to kill' policy were revealed in a recent data leak, and having been repeatedly denied access to the region, the UN High Commissioner for Human Rights, Michelle Bachelet, was unable to speak with any detained Uyghurs or their families when she was finally granted access.

China's rise has created new global fault lines, characterised as a clash between the West and the Rest, a battle between democratic and authoritarian states, leading some to argue there can be no relationship with the Chinese Communist Government. Yet climate change drives a coach and horses through all of that. In today's complex world, we succeed together or fail apart.

So far we have proven ill-equipped to respond to this new reality. The leadership of recent years – of the strongmen who have emerged around the world and the culture they reflect – is entirely unsuited to the challenges of the times. We need a different approach to leadership.

We must be prepared to act with clarity and tenacity in pursuit of multiple, often conflicting goals. Upholding human rights, democratic freedoms *and* action on climate change are all non-negotiable. These are the 'important principles' that Abraham Lincoln said, 'may and must be inflexible'. But at the same time, we must be able to deploy constant, active, patient diplomacy, openness and dialogue, especially with those with whom we disagree. We need to survive setbacks in order to negotiate our shared challenges in the interests of the many, rather than seek to smash others into submission.

Already in the battle for climate security we can glimpse the future, through young emerging leaders in countries across the world, pioneering advances in education, technology, architecture and finance to solve the climate crisis. Listen to these emerging leaders and the future looks bright. It also looks plural.

In 2015, as the newly appointed Shadow Secretary of State for Energy and Climate Change, I brought together Labour council leaders at a clean energy summit, who together agreed plans to eradicate carbon emissions in most of Britain's major towns and cities by 2050. They were driving this change already through green transport, insulating homes, divesting pension funds and building their own energy sources through solar, wind and hydropower. Many were working with community organisations whose energy cooperatives were proving helpful in providing clean energy and reinvigorating local democracy. This was where I first met a young councillor, Arooj Shah, who would later smash many glass ceilings to become the first female Muslim leader of Oldham Council in the North West of England, as she went door to door signing up local residents to the Big Clean Switch, showing the power of collective action in taking on big energy companies, cutting energy bills and cleaning up the planet. Together, at a time when the national government was slashing subsidies for solar energy and blocking new onshore wind turbines, those local leaders were cutting 10 per cent off the UK's carbon footprint and taking communities with them in the fight.

They reminded me that change can come, even when it feels most hopeless, but as with every revolution it rises up from the coalface, until it finds those in power who can see the potential for change and have the courage to grasp it.

THE TECHNOLOGY REVOLUTION

While those local leaders in Britain – like Leeds' Judith Blake, Bristol's Marvin Rees and Dagenham's Darren Rodwell – were seizing control of the future from their own national government, I visited Silicon Valley to see a different vision emerging, where regional and national governments were developing the cutting-edge technology developments in clean energy that this part of California is now famed for. Companies across the world had only just begun to master Carbon Capture and Storage. Now the world's largest machine, designed to suck carbon dioxide out of the air and turn it into rock, has started running in Iceland. Orca can draw 4,000 tonnes of carbon dioxide out of the air every year and inject it deep underground where a complex process of mineralisation turns it into rock.

I saw small start-ups who were designing battery technology capable of storing mind-blowing amounts of energy. I witnessed the exchange of ideas that led to incredible tech developments taking place between companies who had been enticed to Silicon Valley by a federal government that had used a combination of tax breaks and tough environmental regulations to create a market in innovation. I met the young apprentices at the vanguard of this revolution. The path to net zero is paved with a million climate jobs and they were proud to lead the way.

But they knew too that new technology also has the potential to divide. Take, for instance, one potential solution, solar geoengineering, which seeks to make clouds or particle layers in the atmosphere more mirror-like, effectively throwing the sun's rays back into space. In effect, it creates a global sunshade. What nobody yet knows is how those schemes can be developed to reflect the interests of us all. There are fears, for example, that put into practice it could disrupt the tropical monsoon season. With different countries seeking different amounts of cooling, this is technology that could help some countries while harming others.

We are living through a revolution in technology giving us the power to cause or to conquer the world's problems. The technology we have invented allows satellites in space to be used to prevent lives being lost to tsunamis and extreme flooding. It enables education to be extended to millions simply by connecting to the world wide web. And it enables drones to be deployed on the other side of the world at the touch of a button, killing thousands of people, without ever setting foot on their soil.

Technology can help solve the world's problems, connect and empower us. But whether it does depends on how we respond. Nowhere is that more apparent than in the new frontier: social media.

WELCOME TO THE WILD WEST

In August 2021 as Afghanistan fell to the Taliban I was serving as the UK's Shadow Foreign Secretary, overwhelmed with desperate requests from people in Afghanistan in serious danger amidst the chaos of the rushed evacuation. One night, I was live on the BBC from my loft, via the wonders of Skype, talking about the thousands of people who had assisted our efforts in the country over two decades. They were now a target for the Taliban but were hitting a brick wall when they sought help from the Conservative Government. These were children separated from parents, Afghan women MPs being hunted door to door and Embassy staff turned back at the airport for lack of official papers connecting them to Britain – papers which would have got them killed if they had tried to carry them through hastily constructed Taliban check-points. That evening, as I described what was unfolding, a BBC employee in Afghanistan, who was encountering similar bureaucratic hurdles, saw me on TV and reached out for help via email while I was live on air.

The era of social media has opened up possibilities that were the stuff of science fiction back in 1979, the year I was born. That was the year the Walkman was invented, a clunky piece of kit that provided the soundtrack to my childhood. It was an era before Google, before emails, before the internet was even invented. It would be 1994 before two world leaders, Bill Clinton and the Swedish Prime Minister Carl Bildt, exchanged emails for the first time. Now nearly 4.5 billion people – 60 per cent of the world – can connect in an instant.

The experience of young people in the Arab Spring, like the pro-democracy campaigners in Hong Kong and the brave women of Belarus, has shown how technology can be used as a force for liberation, their voices amplified around the world from bedrooms and living rooms instantaneously.

Their experiences show, too, how social media can be used as a tool of repression.

Unsurprisingly, autocratic regimes have seen the restrictive potential of this most powerful of mediums. In China, Google and Facebook operate to standards set by the Government, which restricts who can and can't access information, and sets limits on what can be seen. The Hong Kong authorities imprison those who use social media to speak out in defence of democracy.

But even in democratic countries these new technologies are not always a force for good. A 2019 report from Freedom House claimed nine in ten of us are monitored online.[20] Russia uses cyber attacks and social media to spread disinformation, influence the outcome of elections, sow division and attack democracy. Here in the UK, the Government has used social media to monitor thousands of political activists, many of whom have no criminal background, and was heavily criticised in the pandemic for refusing to release data about public contracts awarded.

The personal data created by social media is a gold mine. It has been used to build a handful of companies that exceed $3 trillion in market value. Imagine for a moment what could be done if that data was used – with our permission – for people instead of profit? Giving individuals the right to decide that their data and technology is used for the common good, could open up endless possibilities, speeding up scientific advancement and human knowledge. Already in medicine there are people seizing the initiative, like those profiled by Mark Stevenson in his eye-opening book *We Do Things Differently*. He describes doctors who have come together to put patients at the centre of research, and patients who have used the possibilities opened up by the internet to share information, creating new cures for debilitating illness. These are just two examples of people using their collective power to advance human knowledge and in doing so pointing us towards that future which James Burke glimpsed almost forty years ago.

Yet, while so much of the political debate concerns the use and ownership of public goods like mail, rail and water, little attention has been paid to the concentration of data and technology in just a few hands. In 2019 the challenge came, not from politicians, but the musician and activist Will.I.Am, who told the 'data monarchs and the next generation of leaders ... to put their energies into data and [Artificial Intelligence] that serve humanity first, instead of designing platforms bent on controlling humanity with money as the primary goal'.

FOR BETTER OR WORSE

But that same technology has opened up the possibility for people, not just elites, to use new forms of technology for ill as well as good. The gatekeepers have been swept away – editors and reporters no longer control what constitutes 'news'. The circulation of national print newspapers has been collapsing since the mid-1990s, and since 2005 over 250 local newspapers have closed in the UK alone. Instead, today half of all adults in the UK get their news from social media. Facebook has 2.4 billion active users – around a third of the world's population. It has opened up to millions of us information that is uncensored but also unverified. Fake news is shared online so often that trust is in short supply and universal truth is up for grabs.

Technology has allowed many of us to be heard. People can also be silenced. Social media is infamous for its bullying and bots but the wall of noise also encourages people to move to the extremes in order to be heard, drowning out moderation, pulling us apart and polarising us.

I felt this acutely after the EU Referendum when the quiet majority, who wanted an end to the division, were frequently drowned out by the noisy extremes. I lost count of how many of my parliamentary colleagues were awake late into the night staring at angry – often threatening – emails, tweets and Facebook posts which invariably hampered the prospect of compromise. Social media creates a dilemma for elected politicians. How to hear the silent majority through the roar of noise? How to protect minority groups and views from what Alexis de Tocqueville called the tyranny of the majority? And how to stand up for what is right? As President Kennedy and Ted Sorensen presciently put it in their 1950s' book *Profiles in Courage*: 'Today the challenge of political courage looms larger than ever before. For our everyday life is becoming so saturated with the tremendous power of mass communication that any unpopular or unorthodox course arouses a storm of protests.'

Imagine what they would have made of the era of social media.

And if it has blown elected representatives off course, it has also thrown other parts of the democratic system, like the traditional media, into disarray. Accepting the 2016 Burton Benjamin Memorial Award for press freedom, CNN's legendary reporter Christiane Amanpour described it like this: 'It appeared much of the media got itself into knots trying to differentiate between balance, objectivity, neutrality, and crucially, truth. We cannot continue the old paradigm – let's say like over global warming, where 99.9 per cent of the empirical scientific evidence is given equal play with the tiny minority of deniers.

'I learned long ago, covering the ethnic cleansing and genocide in Bosnia, never to equate victim with aggressor, never to create a false moral or factual equivalence, because then you are an accomplice to the most unspeakable crimes and consequences. I believe in being truthful, not neutral. And I believe we must stop banalizing the truth.'

The ripple effects from technological advance have created stormy waters and we have not yet discovered how to chart them. But we have been here before.

THE SILICON VALLEY OF THE FIFTEENTH CENTURY

In the 1400s, the invention of the printing press upended society, proving a great leveller and a great disrupter. More books were published in the fifty years after the printing press was invented than in the 1,000 years before. According to

Elizabeth Eisenstein, author of *The Printing Press as an Agent of Change*, within a few decades a printing press could be found in every sizeable community, creating a start-up culture similar to that found in the energy world today. Writing in 1979, before the spread of the internet, she would describe Venice, with its dense cluster of print shops, as the Silicon Valley of its age.

The sheer volume of books produced made suppression far more difficult. The gatekeepers lost their power as people gained it. This put the idea of universal truth up for grabs, allowed ideas to spread and authority to be challenged. Contrary to popular myth, Martin Luther succeeded in challenging the supremacy of the Catholic Church not by nailing his proclamation to a door but by mass-producing and circulating it across the world. Some 300,000 copies were distributed in just three years.

The printing press not only enabled the Reformation but sparked the Enlightenment, extended democracy and put power in people's hands. But as Edward Snowden would later say, 'technology doesn't have a Hippocratic Oath' and so the power that was used to inform, empower and enlighten was also used to spread misinformation, chaos and slaughter.

In an interview with *The Atlantic* just before Eisenstein's death, a journalist recounts how, 'after listening to Betty Eisenstein lay out the wide array of unintended consequences of the printing press, whether mind-altering in a positive or catastrophic way, I made a remark along the lines of "And it took a mere 500 years for things to settle down." "Have they?" she replied.'

The full implications of the technology revolution on the twenty-first century are as difficult to predict as they were in the past. But the question facing us, as it faced the people of the fifteenth century, is how we harness new technologies for our collective benefit. To resolve that, it is necessary to ask: who holds power, and for what ends?

THREE LEADERS, ONE CONSENSUS

In 1979 three very different world leaders set in train major changes in the global economy, which would shift the power dynamic, stripping people across the world of their power and agency and laying the seeds of the major political upheaval on both sides of the Atlantic three decades later.

That was the year Deng Xiaoping opened up China's economy to the world. Within four decades China's economy would go from being one of the smallest in the world to five times the size of the UK, the top trading partner of 120 countries in the world, and the pre-eminent manufacturing power in the world.

It was a necessary response to a major political problem. Decades of communist control had failed to give Chinese workers their share of what they produced. As the baby boomers matured, China had a real problem – huge increases in working-age populations who were about to experience the same low living standards as their parents. Without reform the country risked social and political instability. China could not continue to lag behind the world.

That same year, Margaret Thatcher came to power in the UK, joined just a year later by Ronald Reagan across the Atlantic. Elected amidst a backdrop of high inflation, high unemployment and the demands of millions of workers for better pay and conditions, together they forged a partnership that would sow the seeds of our current crisis. The consensus they built was based on free trade and 'flexible' labour markets that would supposedly grow the economy. The phrase 'a rising tide lifts all boats' was coined to convince us that in this laissez faire world we could all be better off.

The approaches taken by these three leaders, in different circumstances and for different reasons, were to change for the worse the working lives of people in their own countries and across the world. The relative success of working people in places like Wigan and Wuhan now depends to a large extent on global processes and structures that didn't even exist until the 1970s and 1980s.

While China became the pre-eminent manufacturing power, the UK and the USA shifted from industrial to service-based economies. By the mid-1990s the transition was complete but the warning lights were already flashing. A little-noticed but unprecedented rise in the number of people classed as 'economically inactive', or sick, was underway and by the 1990s over 2 million people in Britain were claiming some kind of incapacity benefit – three times as many as in 1979. This was the era when the consensus over the welfare state – that public spending was for public good – broke down and the argument for full employment was lost. Margaret Thatcher's decision to shift the focus of the economy from controlling unemployment to controlling inflation was a settlement that would be tacitly accepted by successive governments, ushering in four decades of economic conservatism.

In 1997 the Labour Party returned to power in Britain facing a choice: to adapt to economic change or to challenge it. The decision to choose to adapt to globalisation – or 'modernisation' as it often became known – was one followed by many governments around the world and it was game-changing for many young people who were handed opportunities that were previously off limits. It allowed Britain to amplify its power around the world and to lead the global charge on issues that deeply affected us, like climate change. But the decision to adapt to economic change rather than challenge it inevitably resulted in winners and losers. 'You can no more debate globalisation', said Tony Blair in 2005, 'than debate whether autumn follows summer. The future belongs to those swift to adapt, slow to complain, open, willing and able to change.' To protect the losers, large scale redistribution was targeted at particular groups – especially pensioners and poorer children. But for those who could not adapt, the future felt much less hopeful. I have been struck by how differently the 'winners' and 'losers' of this era see this moment. If 1979 was a decisive year – representing the birth of a new era of individualization and an assault on the security of working people – 1997 was the moment when, for so many of the casualties of globalisation, the political route to a different future felt like it was closing.

This moment created huge differences in the lived experiences of entire places, starting a process of geographical polarisation. The expansion of university education opened up once-in-a-generation opportunities for many young people and boosted parts of the UK in the process. Today large university towns and cities are among the most successful places in Britain, but while they won, coastal and industrial towns lost out. The same trends played out across the developed world, in the USA and many European countries, with similar results. The World Bank admitted this approach would produce inequalities between places but, it declared, to try and spread opportunity, 'was to fight prosperity not poverty'. Not only had it become clear that a rising tide couldn't lift all boats but now the argument was being explicitly made that it shouldn't. Growth meant casualties, and while progressive governments in the UK and US worked to mitigate the impact of this, for some institutions like the World Bank this was not only inevitable – it was desirable.

Globalisation went up a gear. The advent of global capital flows alongside advances in logistics made it easier for goods and money to move in massive volume across borders. It raised living standards for most, but it also drastically increased inequality. Global wealth grew by 66 per cent between 1995 and 2014[21] and global poverty has been falling consistently for decades. But again, the warning lights flashed. The richest 1 per cent of people now hold as much wealth as nearly 7 billion others. Half the world lives on less than $6 a day and inequality is increasing for more than 70 per cent of the world's population. There are more billionaires now than at any point in human history, but also the sharpest levels of inequality between rich and poor.

This was a settlement that confined workers within their national borders but broke down the barriers that allowed capital to move unimpeded. For the skilled and mobile, free movement became easier, but for many, it was just another excuse for national governments not to invest in them.

This was not an accident of the system. It was the system. 'The winners didn't want to share their gains with the losers,' wrote the Nobel Prize winning economist Joseph Stiglitz. 'Indeed, they liked it that wages were pressured down as American workers had to compete with workers from developing countries. It increased corporate profits all the more.'[22]

This was a visceral illustration of a system that serves profit before people. It enabled manufacturing jobs to be moved around an imaginary chess board by remote and unaccountable powers. Capital moved to wherever profit was most readily found, and it was this that sparked the race to the bottom in working standards and living conditions.

While China was becoming the factory of the world, the UK lost 6 million manufacturing jobs from the 1970s. This process had profound consequences. Most of those jobs were lost from former industrial towns and cities which had once been home to family-owned companies that helped sustain the fabric of the community. And while it dramatically improved living standards for some Chinese citizens, for many workers the wealth they generated was handed over to state-owned manufacturers and developers, meaning their living standards barely improved.

This was an implicit compact between the Chinese Communist Government, global finance and conservative governments in the UK and US, that would eventually, four decades later, lead to that striking moment when the last leader of a major communist government, Xi Jinping, would stand up at the World Economic Forum in Davos in 2017 to defend economic globalisation, which was by then under attack from a US President, Donald Trump.

Their common ground was the need to depress the wages of a skilled workforce and diminish their rights. Growth and profit were the sole objectives and so the security, rights and living standards of workers in places like Wigan and across the world became a problem to be solved, not a right to be realised. Between them they extracted every inch of profit from globalisation.

Over this time, as the French economist Thomas Piketty has documented, economic power shifted from labour to capital. In his book, *Capital in the Twenty-First Century*, Piketty reveals the staggering fact that the richest 1 per cent appropriated 60 per cent of the increase in US national income between 1977 and 2007. This has wider ripple effects, diminishing not just people's incomes but their choices too. As Martin Wolf put it in a review of Piketty's book, 'if as the ancient Athenians believed, participation in public life is a fundamental aspect of human self-realisation, huge inequalities cannot but destroy it'.[23] This democratic deficit is not just a result of growing inequality but a structural problem. This is a world where cars are made in five different countries, with parts criss-crossing the globe until they are made, leaving the workers who build them to function as cogs in a machine which they have no part in shaping. 'Higher efficiency has not been gained without social cost,' noted Michael Young in a 1950s' pamphlet that served an early warning about the challenges of globalisation. 'There is no salvation', he wrote, 'in going back to some misty past in which the small man lived in a small world.' But he pinpointed a central problem: how to exert democratic rights or share a sense of common purpose when decisions are made at a global level. 'The individual', he wrote, 'is only too likely to be and to feel powerless and insignificant.' The challenge is how to build new frameworks for global cooperation, based on democratic consent and shared goals – or what he called a more 'complete' democracy.[24]

The China model creates growth by depressing living standards and flooding the world with cheap goods which are absorbed onto UK and US markets. It is often hailed as good for consumers, but in the shadows you can glimpse the darker side of this pact. As living standards have fallen further, and people have begun to ask who is to blame, populist politicians have moved into this space, pitting worker against worker – Chinese against American, British against European.

This was an era when goods became cheaper, growth was plentiful, but lives became less secure and the seeds of division, within and between countries, were sown.

THE END OF DEMOCRACY?

Today, as Marx predicted, companies are more powerful than nation states, and democratic government is weak in the face of such power. The American company Walmart now controls the twenty-fifth biggest economy in the world, roughly equivalent to Norway's GDP.

A few years ago, I was in a chemist in a former pit village in Wigan campaigning for the pharmacy grant – which subsidised small chemists to enable them to serve smaller communities – to be restored after it had been slashed by the government. A man came in to get some flu medication but the pharmacist couldn't supply them. I asked whether restoring the grant would help and he explained that the real problem was that one of the few companies licensed to distribute drugs in the UK also owned Boots, and with a shortage of flu drugs the local pharmacy was automatically last in the queue. So, on a bitterly cold day, a man in his eighties had to get two buses into the town centre to get his prescription and there was nothing he, or I, could do about it. When did we collectively decide to hand so much power to a corporation based in America, accountable only to its shareholders?

A compact that began in 1979 has created companies that are now truly global entities, shifting the power balance from nation states to them. Multinationals can routinely shift production between countries, creating a race to the bottom as politicians water down workforce rights, wages and taxes to attract them. They mask their activities in tax havens, escaping fair taxation and costing those same communities investment in infrastructure and public services. Money is leaking out of the system. Companies like Amazon pay a lower level of tax than the average worker, with the willing complicity of the democratically elected governments that are supposed to represent them. They also call the shots in terms of regulation. Take Uber, who can threaten to drive down standards, and will get away with it for as long as the mayors of major cities around the world remain divided in their response.

It is anti-democratic in a multitude of ways. The City of London harbours so much illicit finance that sustains authoritarian regimes that it has been dubbed the London Laundromat. But even as UK politicians proclaim the need to stand up for democracy overseas, reform is resisted on the basis that London must retain its status as the global financial centre, in the face of competition from elsewhere. No wonder global happiness is falling and freedom is in retreat. It is too easy for multinationals to appropriate power because nations are divided, not unified, in action.

This is a state of affairs that, in liberal democracies, has left people without control, power or freedom over their own lives. It is felt by many as a tyranny. But, increasingly, some are finding their voice. In 2016, in both the United States and the UK, seismic political earthquakes were sparked by those who were the casualties of this pact, and politicians have had to respond. In Britain the Johnson Government was elected on a short-lived promise to 'level up' the places that had been written off, while President Biden introduced the Inflation Reduction Act, a $700bn investment in domestic energy production and manufacturing and persuaded G20 countries to introduce a global minimum corporation tax to begin to bring an end to this race to the bottom, promising to restore democracy and pursue a foreign policy for the American middle class.[25] The SPD won the 2021 German elections by promising to restore dignity to those who had been 'disrespected' and written off by their government, while in France the 'gilets jaunes' movement prompted President Macron to promise reform, saying 'it is as if they have been forgotten, erased. This is forty years of malaise that has risen to the surface. It goes back a long way, but it is here now.'

Most of these efforts are limited in scope and ambition and do little to disturb the existing power balance. But there is at least a long overdue recognition that politicians must respond to the anger created by a status quo that has robbed people of the power, agency and freedom that rightly belong to them. What happens next is up to us.

The struggle for the future is still playing out. The lesson from those brave young people fighting for freedom during the Arab Spring is that progress is not inevitable. Anger can bring people together to force change, but as we saw in Britain during the EU Referendum, it can also be utilised as a potent force to divide. But there is no challenge to which the answer is more division, anger or walls. So where does that leave Britain?

3.

POPULISM, PATRIOTISM AND POWER

'One cannot see the modern world as it is unless one recognizes the overwhelming strength of patriotism, national loyalty. In certain circumstances it can break down, at certain levels of civilization it does not exist, but as a positive force there is nothing to set beside it.'

George Orwell

It is 2017 and journalists are assembled at the launch of the Labour Party's manifesto in London. A BBC journalist stands up to ask a question and is booed by activists in the room. The Labour leader politely asks them to stop before adding, 'You've noticed some of the media are slightly biased against the Labour Party.'

Welcome to the age of populism.

'A thin-centred ideology', as the academic Cas Mudde puts it, 'that considers society to be ultimately separated into two homogenous and antagonistic camps, "the pure people" versus "the corrupt elite"'.

Across the world, in just a few years – on both left and right – this leapt from fringe protest to shaping mainstream political debate. From the Tea Party and Occupy Wall Street in the USA, to Marine Le Pen's National Rally in France, the Alternative for Germany (AFD), Syriza in Greece and the Indignados and Podemos in Spain, populist movements and parties shook the foundations of traditional party systems, and populist strong-man leaders – Modi, Trump and Bolsonaro – were elected in some of the most powerful countries in the world.

Within a few short years, mainstream political leaders in the UK would routinely frame themselves as for the people, against the elites. This framing, pitting MPs, journalists, civil servants and the judiciary against the people, continued to unfold in Britain even after the assassination of the young MP Jo Cox by a far-right activist in the street. Verbal attacks against civil servants became the norm, the BBC became a regular target, and the front page of one national newspaper labelled the judiciary 'the enemies of the people'.[1]

So when the British Prime Minister Theresa May stood outside Downing Street in March 2019 a line was crossed that at the time, to me, felt like a point of no return: 'You, the public, have had enough. You're tired of the infighting, you're tired of the political games and the arcane procedural rows, tired of MPs talking about nothing else but Brexit when you have real concerns about our children's schools, our National Health Service, knife crime. You want this stage of the Brexit process to be over and done with. I agree. I am on your side. It is now time for MPs to decide.'

In the aftermath of the EU Referendum of 2016, MPs were pulled apart by a tug of war between two opposing groups in the country, half of whom wanted to remain and half of whom wanted to leave. We were constantly warned that we were ignoring the 'the will of the people' but this cheap framing of corrupt MPs versus the pure citizens ignored the truth: MPs were divided because people were divided.

Every day I – like so many others – would wake up to find new death threats in my inbox, at my office and at my home. On one occasion a man arrived in my constituency office threatening my staff with a hammer. Terms like 'traitor' and 'betrayal', largely unheard in British political debate, came to dominate our discourse inside Parliament and were then reflected back to us in the streets of Britain. At a rally in Parliament Square, while effigies of Sadiq Khan, the mayor of London, and the prime minister, Theresa May, were dragged through the streets, I was surrounded by a mob and physically threatened as I tried to get inside to vote.

How did we get here? How did we come so fast to a place where a dangerous culture, so alien to our political traditions, could spread like wildfire?

THE ROAR THAT LIES ON THE OTHER SIDE OF SILENCE

Wind back to 2015 during the EU Referendum campaign and the communities in Britain where voting Labour had once been part of the DNA that ran through people's families. The phrase 'My dad would turn in his grave if I didn't vote Labour' was a common refrain in towns that had returned Labour MPs for a hundred years.

It was in those places, outside the major cities, where the pleas of the Labour leadership to back the Remain campaign rang most hollow. As Will Jennings and Gerry Stoker have documented, anti-politics sentiment, on the rise since World War II, coupled with economic decline, created powerful tail winds that formed the backdrop to the Referendum: between 1997 and 2015, support for leaving the EU more than doubled amongst those living outside cities. It took less than twenty years for Britain's towns to transition from seeing the EU as part of the solution to part of the problem.

These were the places where populist parties, like UKIP (the UK Independence Party), were already finding fertile ground. Between 2010 and 2015, UKIP quadrupled its national vote. In Wigan it leapt from less than 6 per cent of the vote to almost 20 per cent. Its success was just the latest in a series of smoke signals, another sure sign all was not well in our broken political system. But while the electorate sounded the alarm, too many people with power took all the wrong cues.

So many politicians saw the sudden and dramatic rise in support for UKIP as a sign that large sections of the public were now racist and xenophobic but missed how – in so many of those same towns – people had consistently rejected the BNP and openly racist parties for a century. Turnout at elections had been falling for years before this, but it was mistaken for apathy, not anger, because political leaders couldn't hear, as George Eliot put it, 'that roar which lies on the other side of silence'. Reports were commissioned to understand the apathy that had supposedly taken hold instead of any basic effort to listen to what people were trying to tell us. Then came Brexit – largely unanticipated by Parliament, political parties and the media because they had become so deeply disconnected from so many of the people they were meant to represent.

Many of the places where a majority voted to leave the EU were the same places where, over four decades, industries had been lost and with them a sense of place and pride. Towns that within living memory had powered the world through the mines, mills and factories of Britain had experienced decades of economic decline. And that decline coincided with a huge expansion of university education, which was genuinely transformative for many young people, who grasped the opportunities it afforded and left. For those who remained, life felt very different.

This deeper sense of loss is encapsulated for me in the demise of the Upper Morris Street Working Men's Club in my constituency: the headquarters for my first election campaign in 2010. Once a thriving hub in the community, the collapse of the mining industry, and the replacement of the nearby rugby league stadium with a Tesco, led to its decline. Eventually it was demolished, prompting a flood of memories on local Facebook pages from apprentices who found their first job at the club to couples who held their wedding receptions there. Now almost every Labour club in Wigan has closed. These were the shared institutions that, as the Conservative MP Jesse Norman has written, 'shape us as we help to shape them'.[2] Today, on that site stands a busy McDonalds employing young people on minimum-wage, zero-hours contracts.

This is the impact that decisions of recent decades have had on our communities and our sense of belonging, sweeping away the familiar, and with it, as Paul Kingsnorth puts it, our 'mooring in space and time'. But in the political arena, it was barely up for discussion. The conviction that this was not a choice but an inevitability was set out with typical clarity by the then prime minister Tony Blair in 2005 when he told the Labour Party Conference: 'I hear people say we have to stop and debate globalisation. You might as well debate whether autumn should follow summer … The character of this changing world is indifferent to tradition. Unforgiving of frailty. No respecter of past reputations. It has no custom and practice. It is replete with opportunities, but they only go to those swift to adapt, slow to complain, open, willing and able to change.'

These changes ushered in a consensus that would outlast the New Labour Government, built on an economic model that drove investment into previously neglected cities to create growth. By focusing investment, power and opportunities into the big metropolitan centres the hope was some of the benefits would trickle out to surrounding towns. But while, at its best, this approach dragged those towns along in the wake of metropolitan prosperity, for too many people it was an experience of loss and decline, accelerated by the Cameron government in 2010 as they paired this city growth model with deep cuts to public spending.

As life grew harder, less secure and less hopeful, it fuelled a powerful sense that people were ignored by those who ruled them, whether they were hundreds of miles away in Westminster or hundreds of miles away in Brussels. This was a system that not only felt unresponsive but deeply uninterested and at times downright disrespectful towards the priorities for many communities across Britain – rootedness, stability and contribution. This was the backdrop to the EU Referendum.

In the last decade I've found the same loss of trust in politics in parts of Germany, France and Austria outside of the big urban centres where people are more distant from power. It is felt acutely in places where decades of relative decline force young people to move away for lack of good jobs. For some, there are opportunities they willingly grasp. But for so many the choice is between the future, work and opportunity, or home and family. With them has gone the spending power that sustained the community. The scars are visible in the boarded-up high streets and lost community pubs and Post Offices, in the bus networks that are no longer viable. Young people are forced to get out to get on, leaving the places they come from to seek opportunity elsewhere. It has left people growing old alone, hundreds of miles from children and grandchildren, and has written off entire places. What is the point of politics, if these are questions that are handed to the market to decide, no longer even deemed worth including in the political debate?

In 2016, in the aftermath of the EU Referendum, I visited Hilary Clinton's Presidential Election campaign headquarters in New York. Her aides were keen to understand the drivers behind the UK decision to leave the EU. I described the divisions that had grown up between younger, university-educated urban voters and the older, working-class voters who together had propelled Labour to power on three occasions in the last century. Brexit had smashed that coalition to pieces.

The academic Will Jennings and my co-founder, along with the political analyst Ian Warren, of the Centre for Towns, has described these as 'two Englands', each with their own distinct set of attitudes and outlooks: one that believes the future will be better than the past, the other that the past was better than the future.[3]

The Democrats in the United States had long been aware they had a rural problem, and Clinton herself had put time and resources into touring those areas throughout her long campaign. But 'the difference between us and you', remarked one young Clinton aide, 'is that our blue-collar workers have nowhere else to go'.

A few months later, the US electorate put paid to that idea when 100,000 voters, predominantly in rural parts of swing states, switched from Democrat to Republican and gifted Donald Trump the presidency. That part of the electorate, who it was widely assumed had 'nowhere to go', had triggered political earthquakes on both sides of the Atlantic. The divisions could no longer be ignored. 'Populous urban centres' voted for Hillary Clinton by a factor of almost 2:1 – the same ratio by which voters in Britain, living in similar urban centres, voted to Remain. Both Britain and America now contained two countries living uneasily side by side that had lost the ability to understand one another.

THE FLAMES LICKING AT THE SIDES OF LIBERAL DEMOCRACY

Still now, it is little understood how close liberal democracies came to collapse in those years. A system that shrugs its shoulders and says 'this is progress' as the social fabric unravels is not one that gives representation to those affected, and a representative democracy that does not provide representation cannot survive.

If you stop to think about it, representative democracy is remarkable. We allow others to make judgments and decisions on our behalf about things that directly affect the future of our family, community, country and planet. For most people this is trust placed in a political party, not the candidate on the ballot, but still – to hand the right to decide matters of life and death to a person that in most cases you have never met is as much a leap of faith as it is a judgment call. Trust is the glue that holds it together.

So, when growing numbers look to political parties, to Parliament, town halls, civic organisations and the media and too often feel that they work against them, not for them – when they believe their function is to stop people from doing things, or take things away from them, rather than enable them to live richer, larger, more dignified lives; when they can find no expression of these feelings within the system – that is when that trust, that glue, is gone. A survey in 2019 found that low levels of trust, previously found amongst Leave voters and those with fewer qualifications – the losers from the economic system – were now felt across the board. In

England, trust in MPs fell, the further from Westminster you travelled. Burnley in Lancashire recorded the lowest levels of trust, while Hampstead and Kilburn registered highest.[4] This is the fertile ground that populism feeds on, that belief that the interests of the elites are directly pitted against those of the people. There are, as academics Harry Pitts and Matt Bolton put it, 'those on both left and right who luxuriate in the flames licking at the sides of liberal democracy',[5] and it is an existential challenge.

For all the anger and division this age of populism has created, it has been populist movements that have allowed people to sound the alarm, to give voice to real grievances and to shine a spotlight on a system that has gone badly wrong. It has revealed a political system wholly unequipped to respond. As divisions widened, institutions that were meant to bring us together and mediate difference failed. The spaces for politics shrunk into spaces for protest. Consider the way Brexit descended into insults and slanging matches across the media, Parliament and within our political parties. Where are the spaces in those systems and institutions to bring people together? In Parliament, committee rooms are separated by barriers, the chamber by division lines. Even the Members' tearoom, a legendary place where MPs often gather between votes, is divided into party sections. As a result there are very few physical spaces where people can sit together and thrash out the common ground. And like a pressure cooker that overheated, populism provided the safety valve.

SUBVERT, DISTORT, DIVIDE

But that is as far as it takes us because, far from providing answers, populism subverts, distorts and divides. The two major Brexit campaigns – Vote Leave and the People's Vote

– were near perfect examples of how the willingness to embrace populist rhetoric ultimately ends up wrecking democratic debate. Offering simplistic solutions – 'Just leave with no deal!' or 'Have another referendum!' – on the promise the question would be settled and we could easily move on, they admitted of just one right and one wrong answer. But the problem of a deeply divided nation and the many heartfelt views on Brexit, and all the things Brexit had come to symbolise, were not going to vanish. They are complex, demanding of nuance and still, even now, will not be wished – or voted – away.

Populism cannot help resolve this. It obscures rather than enlightens. It reduces democracy to a tug of war in which might is right, on the false premise that one side can win while the other must inevitably lose. It offers no explanation about how change is made in politics, shuts people out of the process and shakes our faith in each other and the system. It ignites rage and provokes blame but misdirects that energy and in doing so prevents much-needed change.

We have to do better.

THE COUNTRY THAT LIES BENEATH THE SURFACE

And we can. This is not an age of anger, as it has been compellingly described by the author Pankaj Mishra, but one of hope. The anger he documents across the world is real, but it is born not from despair but from the certain belief that things can and must be better.

A few years ago, I visited Grimsby – a place where large numbers had voted to leave the EU – to see what had become of the fishing industry, whose decline had become a major focus for Leave campaigners. I found a group of people there who had remodelled their industry with great ingenuity and were now exporting fish products to the world. But it was down the road that I caught a glimpse of the future. Thanks to the foresight of local leaders and the regional development agency of well over a decade ago, companies from all over the world have been persuaded to invest in Grimsby because of its great natural asset – wind. That has created good, skilled work and a palpable sense of contribution to Britain's energy needs and the fight against climate change. I met young apprentices glowing with pride as they showed me around the factory floor. According to the government's own climate advisors the number of people on benefits in Grimsby has halved in the last decade thanks to this one industry alone and by 2030 Grimsby will be powering most of the north of England. Places like Grimsby are often remarked on by national policy-makers for the problems they pose, but closer to home people see only potential. They demand a national plan that is as ambitious for their place as they are.

Take the East Marsh area of Grimsby, which ranks among the 1 per cent most deprived estates in the country.[6] Many of the young people who could, grasped the opportunities opened up to them, and left to seek opportunity elsewhere. Those who remain are – according to a 2011 study – among the most 'disengaged' in the country. No wonder communities who had effectively been written off by commentators and their own national government found such resonance in the phrase 'Take Back Control'. But for all of the challenges they face, there is power in these communities. On the East Marsh estate in Grimsby, residents formed a community group, East Marsh United, to rebuild their community, draw in investment and match the ambition of their young people. Together they have connected young people to jobs and opportunities, bought housing stock to create decent homes and raise revenue and invested back in the community. It is a remarkable journey that has gained them national recognition but they embarked on it in the certain knowledge that if change was coming, they must lead it themselves.

This is the country that, as George Orwell wrote, 'lies beneath the surface',[7] where people come together in common cause to improve lives and build better. It is driven by a quiet patriotism, a belief and pride in family, community and country. As Orwell said, 'as a positive force there is nothing to set beside it'.

This is the force that is already driving change in the country, pulling people together and spurring us on to solve problems. We saw it during the global pandemic when nurses and care home workers, delivery drivers and council workers went out day after day to keep the country going. Quietly and with no fanfare they put themselves at risk to aid the national effort.

QUIET PATRIOTISM

This is the quiet patriotism that exists across the country, quite different from the noisy brand appropriated by so many politicians who sling pints of real ale for the cameras and demand the flag is displayed prominently at every opportunity all the while supporting the decline of communities and the poverty of their people. Like so many others, I instinctively feel theirs is a false patriotism. As was once said of Oswald Mosley, it is as hollow as a jug.

I grew up in Manchester in the 1980s, a time when racial tensions played out daily on our streets and racial discrimination was openly displayed in the playground and the workplace. For many young people, especially young black men, a toxic mix of racism, unemployment and a lack of expression in the political system had created a perfect storm. It was this that sparked the uprising in 1981 when, as in other major cities such as London, Liverpool and Birmingham, the Moss Side riots briefly set the city alight. Far-right groups were buoyed by a police force who were openly hostile to the young black men in the city. For a mixed-race child like me, in those days the sight of the St George's flag was the equivalent of a sign saying 'not welcome here'. But my multicultural family, friends and neighbours told a different story about the city we belonged to. During the Moss Side riots, my parents worked with other local leaders – white, black and Asian – to turn around national media coverage that was overwhelmingly hostile to the young people of Moss Side and in doing so shone a spotlight on what was really happening.

That's why I have always felt that there was something better to be fought for. A country that doesn't simply tolerate diversity but sees it as its strength. When I look at those brave young England footballers who took the knee – in defiance of their own government – to show solidarity with a global resistance movement against racism, I see the future of our country reflected in their spirit. They look like the young people I grew up alongside in Manchester, but while so many of those young people had no power or platform, the likes of Marcus Rashford and Tyrone Mings have, and by using it they have reclaimed the flag and the values it represents.

This is what quiet patriotism looks like, measured not in the number of our flags but in the health of our children, the strength of our communities, the dignity of our workforce and the security of our nation. One that can turn that strength outwards to stand up for people in the UK and overseas knowing that patriotism is not a zero-sum game, that when you live these values they multiply.

You will find it among our armed forces, proud to serve under our flag with the quiet determination of those who did not hesitate to fly into danger in Afghanistan in the summer of 2021, to stand by those who had stood by us. As the government stepped back, they stepped forward, keeping our promises to thousands of people in Afghanistan in defence of the work they had done alongside the Afghan people over two decades – to clear landmines, save lives and enable millions of girls to go to school.

This is a patriotism that starts from an honest assessment and understanding of who we are and the impact we have had in the world, confident enough to be open about the country's past, and in doing so, learn from it. It is defined by honesty about the history of the Empire, for good and bad, that my dad grew up in, not the PR exercise led by the Conservative Government to rewrite the curriculum and define 'British values'. It is the raw, honest patriotism of the poet Wilfred Owen and his brutal account of war, not the fundamentally dishonest patriotism of a prime minister who praises the armed forces then makes them redundant and leaves veterans on the streets of Britain. Look closely at the photographs of the Jarrow Marchers and you'll see, tucked into their top pockets, slips for war medals that had been taken to be pawned. Any account of the war that refuses to acknowledge that this is how we treated many of our war 'heroes' when they returned has learnt nothing from the past, so has nothing to teach us about the country we can build in the future.

A few years ago I laid out, in Bristol, what we could be if we understood the power in this quiet patriotism:

'As we leave the EU I want to talk to you about the city I stand in and the country we seek to lead.

'A city which was built on the backs of the slave trade that is now led by Europe's first directly elected black mayor.

Whose citizens are showing leadership on climate change and compassion towards refugees.

'This is the Britain we can be.

'A country that remembers where it's been but knows where it's going.

'That knows the path of least resistance has never pointed towards progress.

'When Bristolians boycotted the buses in the 1960s to defeat a company that refused to employ black and Asian drivers they changed our history and they changed mine. My dad arrived in this country in the 1950s from India and fought those battles all his life. It led him to help create the Race Relations Act, one of the greatest gifts Labour has given to this country.

'The Tories say we are "a small island that punches above its weight", never stopping to ask why it is they are punching at all.

A self-confident empowered country we will lead will be different.

'A country where Benjamin Zephaniah can accept the Order of British Excellence, not reject the Order of British Empire. That recognises the contribution of our people, and celebrates, not seeks to alienate, them.'

'One that never accepts the world as it is but strives to build the world as it should be, written as Zephaniah says "in verses of fire".

Patriotism isn't fixed. It evolves like a living, breathing bridge, stretching between the past and the future. That is why it must be built on an honest, inclusive national story. Ours is the history of ordinary, often extraordinary, people who built this country, and tell the stories that only a small few – like the brilliant historian Eric Hobsbawm – have ever tried to tell. It is the history of waves of immigration that have shaped our language, our institutions and our values. It is the history of different values than the ones we are offered by our leaders – not self-interest and individual achievement but of common endeavour and solidarity – and the story of a people who still believe strongly, across class, race and geographical boundaries, in ideals like free speech, the right to a fair trial and the rule of law.

I can only think of one serious attempt to tell this national story in my lifetime: the opening ceremony to the 2012 Olympic Games in London, or as Jonathan Freedland beautifully described it at the time, a 'hymn to collective endeavour'.[8] Headed by a man, Danny Boyle, who had turned down a knighthood because he would rather be an equal citizen than a preferred subject, it captured the messy, complicated and some-times conflicted country we live in. 'It didn't seek to airbrush the darkness in our history,' writes Freedland. 'It was able to speak openly about the country's strengths and weaknesses.'

As Danny Boyle describes it, the participants were told 'this is the people's show and you're lucky to be in it'. He took 10,000 volunteers who, with incredible symbolism, rehearsed in the car park of the abandoned Ford plant at Dagenham. Unlike modern Hollywood sets there were no privacy contracts, no mobile phones were confiscated, and not a single image leaked before the opening night. Together they didn't just portray those values, of collectivism, solidarity and common ties – they lived them. Boyle told the *Guardian* it couldn't have succeeded if it was simply a left-wing view of Britain. It was based on values that are fundamental to so many of us. 'When it comes to institutions like the NHS,' he says, 'we decided long ago that "we believe in that".'

Just a couple of years later the UK was rocked by a referen-dum in which nearly half of all Scots voted to break up the

United Kingdom, and the entire country was beset by division during the EU Referendum and its aftermath. When I sat down to talk to Danny Boyle in 2019 to reflect on the upheaval of recent years, we met fittingly in Toynbee Hall in London, which gave the people of the East End a voice and provided a home to some of the great reformers of recent centuries, like Clement Attlee and William Beveridge. We reflected on that opening ceremony, which pulled the nation together in a collective story of common achievement, and I asked him, where did that country go? 'It's still there,' he told me. 'It's just waiting for someone to give it a voice.'

When I think of any great British achievement – the National Health Service, the war effort, the Race Relations Act, comprehensive education, the world's first climate change act or the minimum wage – I think not of one person but of many. These were things that could only come into being because of a belief that, by the strength of our common endeavour, we achieve more than we achieve alone. This is the patriotism I believe in, different to nationalism, as Peter Hain says 'a noble value not a narrow one'[9] that brings people together in common cause instead of driving them apart.

Over the course of my lifetime we've seen more and more of a focus on heroic individuals, from Harvey Milk to Malala Yousafzai – all amazing, inspiring people – but somewhere along the way we've forgotten that nothing worth doing was ever done alone. It's movements that change things, or in the words of Ernest Hemingway's great literary hero Harry Morgan, 'one man alone ain't got no bloody chance'.[10] For all the divisions of recent times, we are all, whether we like it or not, Aristotle's political animals, deeply social with a desire to be different but a deeply held human need to belong. 'Every man,' he wrote 'by nature, has an impulse towards others.' We find our identity through the things we have in common, at the football match, the church group, marching in common cause, in our universities and the workplace. Through our teams, our friends or our families, being human means being part of something, defining ourselves for who we are and what we are for, not just what we stand against.

THE INVISIBLE CHAIN

This is why the way so much of the left has come to dismiss or belittle the patriotism on display in towns across Britain is not only curious. It is a disaster. It has abandoned our national story to those who use it to exclude and divide. It has forgone a country that knows what it stands for and that can be honest about, and come to terms with, its past (good and bad), that can see its strengths and weaknesses with equal clarity, and that can include all its citizens.

Most of all, it has ignored something that matters deeply to our collective future. This belief in family, community, country gives us more than an anchor – it gives us a stake. In a moment when people are crying out for rootedness in a world that too often feels it is spinning out of control, turning to populist movements and protest, this is the counter force, the invisible chain that binds the nation together.

This search for a stake in the modern world is not new. This was also the theme picked up by Michael Young in 1949, at a moment of similar rupture after World War II. He warned about the tension between the nature of a globally interdependent modern world and the very human need for a sense of grounding, belonging and agency. He recognised the way in which modern work had uprooted people and communities and cost us a sense of contribution, stake and belonging. No wonder the dramatic rise in English national sentiment eighty years later coincided with the rise of short-term insecure work, the loss of good jobs and the loss of social institutions.[11]

That fertile ground that populists exploit can be countered by restoring power and agency to drive and shape decisions to those who have a stake in them – because institutions that people have a stake in are institutions worth fighting for.

There is a lesson about the power of belonging buried in the official report into the 1981 Moss Side riots. The author, Benet Hytner QC, writes that as the riots progressed through Princess Street in Rusholme, the shopfronts in the path of the demonstrators were smashed, all except the youth centre, which stood alone among them completely untouched.

This should surely tell us that what we have witnessed in recent years is an outcry from people who have learnt that, as Nye Bevan put it, 'silent pain evokes no response'. Even when things seem most bleak or destructive, there is a basis from which to build better.

During the EU Referendum I came to feel that too many of the arguments we put forward as part of the Remain campaign were driven by a sense of pessimism. At their heart was the idea that as a small country we had little to offer, unable to shape the world beyond our shores. If you believe in country, family and community you look first for the strengths across the country that we contribute as allies to the world – whether it's the scientists in Oxford who led the search for a vaccine, or the thousands of minimum wage workers in Britain who donated their own money to ensure it reached every corner of the globe. Long before I was elected to Parliament, my politics was shaped by the homeless teenagers, children in care and child refugees I worked with, who were driven not out of anger that things were so bad, but out of hope that things could be better. Some of those children will stay with me forever. The girl who had been given eight different social workers in three years, moved from placement to placement since entering the care system. She was just nine years old. The young boy who stopped speaking after being locked up in Yarl's Wood Immigration Detention Centre with his mum. The young woman who had been preyed upon by loan sharks, in mountains of debt aged just nineteen and trapped in a hostel. They were angry, hurt and anxious about the future but they never gave up. They are the optimists. We should be too.

POWER

We must harness the belief and ambition that has spurred so many people on, not just to change our country but to change the world.

The age of populism has morphed, at times, into an age of retreat – but retreat is not inevitable. The global pandemic showed us two visions of the future. The moment we needed to come together we saw attacks on the World Health Organisation, a scramble for PPE, the rise of vaccine nationalism and scapegoating of migrants. It led the director general of the World Health Organization to say that 'the biggest challenge we face is not the virus itself, but the lack of solidarity globally and locally'. But even as those geopolitical tensions rose and the politics became increasingly toxic, I Zoomed with brave and brilliant scientists – Chinese and American, British and European – and many others besides who were cooperating across borders, in the case of China often at great personal risk, and together found the vaccines, diagnostics and treatment that have already saved millions of lives. This is the spirit Britain needs to summon for the challenges we face.

This argument – that only by turning outwards can we solve problems closer to home – matters now more than ever.

When Boris Johnson labelled the Department for International Development a giant cashpoint in the sky, abolished the department and slashed its budget, he argued that we cannot both keep our promises to the world and to people at home. This was a variation on a theme developed by his predecessor Theresa May, that you can be for the world or for your country, but not for both.

But the world beyond our shores, and our ability to mould and shape it, affects the lives of people in towns across Britain to an extraordinary degree. Our relationship with China is more central to the factory operative earning £10.90 an hour in Stockton than any high-street grant. Our ability to drive the world towards net zero is central to the future of the café owner in Halifax whose business is beset by frequent flooding. The unregulated world of global finance that allows the likes of Lex Greensill to bet the house on 'get rich quick' schemes directly affects the security of steel workers in towns like Rotherham. Only global action can take on the oligarchs who subvert our democracy, avoid the taxes that fund our schools and hospitals and use the things that matter to us – like football clubs – as playthings.

Almost a century ago the seams of my family were threaded together when the Indian independence campaign, supported by my grandparents in India, had devastating consequences for Lancashire textile workers. When the cotton stopped coming, the mills stopped running and the workers went hungry. But members of my family, who worked in those mills, were among those who welcomed Gandhi to Lancashire. Because they knew, as I know, that solidarity amongst working-class people has power and our struggle is one and the same.

If we want a better country and a better world then we have to defeat those who say that if you believe you are a citizen of the world, you are a citizen of nowhere. We have to show that we will use every local, national and global tool at our disposal to improve the lives of working-class people here *and* across the world. And we should give people ownership of those decisions, to put them in the driving seat with a stake and a voice. Policy is so often discussed and agreed in closed rooms without reference to the people affected and nowhere more so than in foreign policy. The debates are separate. The worlds are disconnected. When was the last time our great foreign policy institutions debated in towns across Britain?

This dangerous gulf that has grown up between foreign and domestic policy has cost support and consent for action in the world and has held us back at home. It has created the space for people like Johnson to believe we can be persuaded to turn inwards, to blame others for our problems instead of doing the hard graft to solve them ourselves. Only a country that is rooted in the interests and priorities of its people, in which we all have a stake, can sustain the support to act as a force for good in the world and earn the support and consent of people at home.

But if people were in the driving seat, seeing clearly the difference we could make, things would change.

A few months ago when violence flared in the Middle East, a national newspaper columnist wrote a piece headlined 'Red Wall voters think Labour cares more about the Palestinians than them. And they're right.' It argued that the working-class older voters who had left Labour in such large numbers were completely alienated by Labour's support for the children killed in Palestine.[12]

I thought of it a few weeks later as I discussed Palestine with some children at a school in Halifax. I'd been asked to visit by the headteacher and popular local MP Holly Lynch because of the strength of feeling amongst many of the children in the school about what was happening in Israel and

Palestine. Those children, some as young as eleven, told me in their broad Yorkshire accents about how heartbroken they were by the airstrikes against people in Gaza. And when I asked them why it mattered so much to them (did they have family there perhaps?) one young girl said to me, 'It hurts us to see it. I feel they're human beings who need help and I also feel they're Muslims like us, and if it was happening to us, we'd want someone to defend us.' None of their passion for what was happening in Palestine made them any less interested in what was happening close to home in Yorkshire, especially in their own school. Nor did it prevent them from being open, interested and concerned either when I talked about the impact of the rocket attacks on Israeli citizens. They wanted to know immediately what I would do then for both Israelis and Palestinians. Just as years ago I learnt how Christianity drove many of my colleagues at the Children's Society to stand by child refugees, I saw at this Yorkshire school how Islam was helping these young people to stand with people overseas, motivated not by what they were against but what they were for. How religion, which can be used to divide, can also be a unifying force if we let it. This sense of global solidarity amongst the children of Yorkshire, some as young as eleven, is how I know the lazy stereotypes about the Red Wall – that people care little for the world beyond our shores – are wrong and thankfully a dead end for politicians who seek to exploit them.

This is what quiet patriotism gives you: a country at ease with itself, that knows what it is for, that can have the confidence to live its values at home and the courage to stand for them in the world. A country that can go out and shed light, not just might, in the world – proud to campaign against the death penalty and fly the Pride Flag over our embassies in countries where love is a crime. A country that invests in its people and puts them at the centre of our vision for the world is, in the end, one that can call itself patriotic, because it is from them that power is derived and to them it must return. As the former Foreign Secretary Ernest Bevin once put it: 'After all the thought you can give to it, the only repository of faith I have been able to find … is the common people.'

4.

A NATION OF WINNERS AND LOSERS

'There have always been ideas worth fighting for.'

People's History Museum

It was the summer of 2018 and I was on the picket line. As the sun beat down during those sweltering weeks, we stood outside Wigan Infirmary with the hospital porters, cleaners and administrators who were out on strike, having tried and failed to persuade managers to drop plans to outsource their jobs to a private company.

The hospital management were racing against the clock to cut costs because of a system, created by government, aimed at forcing down public sector spending. Hospital trusts who cut spending got a financial reward at the end of the year, while those who didn't were hit with a penalty. After a decade of cuts to health funding, and successive rounds of national reorganisation, managers were desperate not to lose more funding and were running short on inspiration.

But over in Gateshead, a few years earlier, hospital bosses had discovered a shortcut that could help them to get to the golden number. By setting up a private, arm's-length company they could claim tax breaks on staff costs that weren't available to the public sector. And so it came to pass that hundreds of the lowest paid, longest serving staff who were the back-bone of our local hospital were told they were being turfed out of the NHS into a new company, named WWL (Wrightington, Wigan and Leigh) Solutions.

They were worried by the experience of hospital staff in other parts of the country who had seen sick pay cut, staff laid off and promises broken. Nobody in the town was a stranger to the impact of outsourcing – our bus drivers, home care and postal workers had all lived through it, and with it the slow destruction of the wages, job security and working conditions that form the basis of a secure life. But more than that, so many of those who stood on that picket line were fighting for an idea – of a healthcare system free at the point of use that they were proud to work for, that they saw not as a job, but a vocation, and that they had invested care and energy in to keep going through good times and bad.

During those long hot weeks we were joined on the picket line by off-duty medical staff, members of the public and even some of the hospital managers – because, like us, this was an ideal they cherished, that they had strived for, and one for which they were prepared to fight. People honked their horns in support as they passed, stopping to drop off bottles of water and thanks. One elderly man told me he couldn't shake the image of his sister who had died as a child – unable to afford GP fees, she had been buried in a pauper's grave.

Those behind the plans argued the opposition was 'irrational'. But in truth we were counting different things. The Government counted the value of money clawed back to the Treasury. The plan's champions were counting the value of the precious funding that could help the NHS to keep delivering for patients in the toughest of times. But, like the staff on the picket line, the elderly man who stopped to talk to us that day was counting the value of an NHS that is open to all because it belongs to all.

The staff were acutely aware of the conundrum, and they wanted to help. They had collectively come up with smart solutions that could only have been devised from the front-line, with some brilliant ideas about how to save on unnecessary costs. Was it really so outlandish that they wanted to be included – not just consulted – in decision making about something they held such a stake in? We all need, want and increasingly demand the right to be included in the decisions enacted on our behalf and I passionately believe that, if we are, those decisions are always better for it.

A handful of trade union officials worked around the clock to keep negotiations going, and at the darkest of times skilfully brought the sparks of hope flickering back to life. We were bolstered by the political support we attracted locally and at the highest levels. But in the end what saved the day was a Labour Council who knew the value of those staff, their job security and the wages that made a significant contribution to the economy of our town – and understood the value of the NHS to the people of Wigan.

As the deadline approached, they stepped in with the funding that would allow the Hospital Trust to avoid a penalty, in return for a focus on closer, community-based health services that took pressure off the hospital and got help to people earlier. As part of the deal, the plans were consigned to history. And only two short years later the whole nation would come to understand and celebrate the value of those porters, cleaners and administrators, as we applauded from our doorsteps those who had stepped into danger during the pandemic, working day and night to save countless lives.

But even as we celebrated, we were acutely aware that our victory was highly unusual. And while we had won the battle, we hadn't won the war. Jobs had been saved but these same staff still work gruelling hours, often long after their shifts have officially ended, for pay that covers less and less of the basic essentials each year. In the Arthur Miller play, *Death of a Salesman*, the hero Willy Loman grinds for a living in the vain hope of achieving a better life, only to be discarded when his employer can no longer extract as much from him. As he loses everything, he shouts into the void: 'You can't eat the orange and throw the peel away – a man is not a piece of fruit!'

For too many people in modern Britain this is the reality. Those porters, administrators and cleaners were victims of a system where risk and insecurity are passed down from government, to management, to the workforce – from those who have the wealth, power and resilience to bear it to those who don't. They are part of an army of people in every part of the UK who are told their contribution simply doesn't count – considered to have less value than figures on a balance sheet – and dismissed as irrational or hopeless nostalgics by self-described 'modernisers' when they object. They and their families have trodden the well-worn path of watching their jobs hived off to private sector companies where unions are weaker, collective bargaining is non-existent and power has shifted overwhelmingly from worker to employers. They deserve far more respect.

Just like the young people in Tunisia we met earlier, they are the casualties of a system that creates winners and losers – the few who hold power and will not relinquish it easily, and the many, many people who are denied a say over the things that matter in their lives, communities and country. For all the advances of recent years, something has gone badly wrong when this is the experience of so many people.

THE SWEATSHOPS OF THE MODERN ERA

The technology revolution and the choices made by British, American and Chinese premiers in the 1980s laid the seeds for the modern world of work. Jobs in the public sector have given way to jobs in the private sector, more likely to be in offices than factories, in services than industry.

Much anguish has been expended about the downsides of automation. But the demise of backbreaking, difficult, dangerous work has been one of the reasons why people can now expect to live on average five years longer than they could in 1979. For many people, especially men, it has meant being able to retire, to meet their grandchildren and spend precious years with their families as, across the country, the mines, mills, factories and steelworks that left us with a legacy of lung and heart disease have made way for jobs in 'services'.

But what services? The manual labour of the industrial age has been replaced with jobs in nail bars, care homes, hair salons and fast food outlets, where workers are predominantly female, young or from minority backgrounds. This is the freelance, temporary world of work known as the gig economy, home to 4.4 million workers in England and Wales alone, one in ten working-age adults.[1] It is fast becoming the defining condition of modern work: in the last few years the gig economy has more or less tripled in size. But it is also characterised by low pay – or in the case of zero-hours contracts, no pay – with employment typically contracted through agencies on short-term contracts, without job security or rights and in poor working conditions. A former Governor of New York caused a storm but caught a mood when he described it as 'the sweatshop of the modern age'.

This is the brutal reality of many modern workplaces, where workers for Amazon – a company valued at £1.4

trillion – describe how they are treated as robots, not people. An investigation in 2022 revealed ambulances had been called out to the company's warehouses 1000 times since 2018. One employee told the investigation, 'Amazon sees people just like numbers, just like rats.' While they toiled for the UK minimum wage of £9.50 an hour, their boss Jeff Bezos made £8.5 million an hour.[2]

No modern country should tolerate this treatment of its people, but the reality for those who try to improve their lot is also bleak. When the GMB trade union successfully challenged Uber's assertion that its 40,000 UK drivers were independent contractors, not workers, the Supreme Court described the power imbalance between the company and its workers: 'Drivers', it noted, 'are in a position of subordination and dependency in relation to Uber such that they have little or no ability to improve their economic position through professional or entrepreneurial skill.'[3]

WHO GAINS?

When he announced what would become a decade of austerity – harsh, deep spending cuts to public services – David Cameron said 'we are all in this together'. But we weren't. Between 2014 and 2018, FTSE 100 companies returned 80 per cent of profits to shareholders. There was a 45 per cent increase in dividends, while share buybacks more than doubled, but at the same time incomes fell by 3 per cent. The Trades Union Congress calculated that if pay across the UK economy had kept pace with shareholder returns, the average worker would be over £9,500 better off. The theory goes that shareholders are exposed to the greatest risk of all business stakeholders – which justifies big dividends when times are good just as, when profits fall, returns to shareholders should fall too. But the TUC found that this was not the case – that whether profits rose or fell, shareholders could expect consistent returns regardless.[4]

The pandemic should have forced us to fundamentally reconsider our economy and who it works for. Instead, the private sector workers who kept our homes heated and our supermarket shelves stocked are denied a fair share of income, wealth or power, and appalling work practices have spread. 'Fire and rehire' is a tactic used to cut costs for shareholders, pushing risk and insecurity onto those who can hardly bear it. An estimated 9 per cent of workers were forced to reapply for their jobs on worse terms after the start of the pandemic.[5] Just as under George Osborne and David Cameron, major cuts to public sector spending (supposedly to reduce the public debt) caused private debt to rise: the risk and the hardship passed from us all, collectively, to individuals.

This was a game of winners and losers. Many individuals lost out, but so too did entire areas. The demise of industry and the loss of 2 million jobs was not evenly distributed across Britain. The workers who are so disadvantaged by the gig economy are more likely to be concentrated in places where industry has departed and where, for too many people, this work is the only game in town.

In many coastal and industrial towns, the factory, steelworks or mines were the only major employer. These were often companies with a strong local presence – like Ford in Dagenham or Rowntree in York – where a relationship between workers and owners was still possible. In some workplaces, this meant a much closer, stronger alliance between owners, managers and workforce. Not only did workers have a stake in the future of the company, but the company had a stake in the future of the town.

It is easy to overstate this. There was no equality in the power relationship for workers – especially women, immigrants and minorities. Progress was long in the making and hard won, as shown by the legendary battles fought by women workers at Grunwick Film Processing in Brent or at Ford in Dagenham. Just to gain union recognition and equal pay, women had to take on management, owners, politicians and sometimes the trade union movement too. The Labour MP Jack Dromey, who was a member of the strike committee at Grunwick, recalls how Jayaben Desai, a fearless Gujarati woman, who led the workers out on strike on another searingly hot day in 1976, told the management who had likened them to 'chattering monkeys', 'what you are running isn't a factory, it is a zoo. But in a zoo there are many types of animals. Some are monkeys who dance on your fingertips. Others are lions who can bite your head off. We are those lions, Mr Manager.'[6]

Ultimately, those Grunwick workers were forced back to work and others were sacked. But over the course of their two-year battle they orchestrated the biggest mobilisation in British Labour movement history and, as Dromey tells it, 'brought home to the big battalions of organised labour an understanding of the grim reality facing' women and immigrant workers, building a solidarity that was unthinkable across the Labour movement before these brave women stood up for what was right. In one of our last WhatsApp exchanges just two days before he died, Jack told me, 'It was a remarkable chapter in the history of the British Labour movement and immigration. Jayaben was a legend and I loved her. She made history.' He was right.

The success of the Grunwick strikers in mobilising 20,000 workers in their defence also reportedly persuaded the Thatcher Government to introduce some of the most restrictive trade union laws in history. Since then, as big local employers have been replaced by multinational organisations whose location is often offshored and who employ workers through subsidiary companies, power has become far more remote and successful collective action far harder. With many companies now more powerful than nation states, the UK Government has been unwilling to take action to rein in the excesses of the gig economy, and people have been turned from contributors to units of capital, to be used or expended at the will or whim of billionaires who have never set foot in the places where their modern sweatshops are based.

THE RISING TIDE

But insecure, low-paid, dehumanising work doesn't give rise only to economic uncertainty – workers also suffer stress, sickness and mental health problems. And besides misery, it's not delivered anything. Britain remains one of the least productive developed economies. Much ink, brainpower and energy has been expended on how to solve what is known as the 'productivity puzzle' – why output per worker in the UK lags stubbornly behind so many other countries. Only for a short time, in the early 1980s, has output per worker matched other comparable economies. Many economists and politicians still chase after the productivity 'miracle' that occurred under the Thatcher Government. Some have framed the issue as one of getting people to work harder, believing that it is a lack of hard graft that holds Britain back. It found its most striking expression in the book *Britannia Unchained*, which argued that Britain was held back by a nation of 'the worst idlers in the world'.[7] It is no coincidence that the five up-and-coming Tory MPs who co-authored it went on to occupy some of the most important offices of state – the prime minister, deputy prime minister and chancellor among them. This point of view had become commonplace within the political establishment. For too long too many have chased after the productivity 'miracle', without challenging the basic assumptions behind the 'productivity puzzle', and politicians of all parties have implicitly accepted the idea that people simply need to put more effort in.

But, as Labour MP Jon Cruddas points out in his book *The Dignity of Labour*, the Thatcher Government didn't stumble across a 'miracle'. They boosted productivity by removing 2 million jobs from the workforce between 1979 and 1982 and sweating the remaining workers harder, extracting from them all they could give. They were 'held back' in this endeavour by trade unions and workplace rights, like sick leave, holiday entitlement and bereavement leave, and so it was in this era that rights became the supposed enemy of productivity and the seeds of the modern workplace were sown.

We haven't just written off the contribution of most people – we've written off the contribution of most places too. For nineteen of the last twenty years, only two regions of the UK – London and the South East – have had the backing and investment to consistently stay in surplus, paying more into the Treasury than they take out.[8] Even without soaring inflation, the pandemic and a paper-thin Brexit deal, this fundamental weakness in the British economy remains. It has deep roots. Estimates of regional GDP per head from a century ago expose the same trend – placing London alone well above the UK average,[9] but Britain is now unique amongst major countries in believing we can power a modern economy using only a handful of people in a handful of sectors in one small corner of the country. This isn't a productivity puzzle, it's a productivity choice and one that isn't working for any of us.

The UK is one of the most geographically unequal countries in the world and with a wider productivity gap than anywhere else in the G7, which costs the UK economy an estimated £50 billion a year.[10] Our core cities lag behind their counterparts in Europe, our regions are struggling and many of our towns and villages are written off altogether. Even the 'winners' are losing. Some 750,000 people move to London every year, seeking new opportunities.[11] Twenty years ago I was one of them. London is the region with the highest disposable incomes by a long stretch until you factor in housing costs, and then people are worse off than most parts of the UK, working longer hours, with lower disposable incomes, air pollution, congestion and soaring rates of poverty.[12]

We have put up with this for too long. What if we ditched these wrongheaded ideas about productivity and learnt to see people and places as partners and contributors to the country's success, not assets to be sweated or problems to be managed? Could the future look brighter? Could it look like a New Deal?

A MILLION CLIMATE JOBS

The Green New Deal is an idea that has gained traction since it was first coined by the *New York Times* columnist Thomas Friedman in 2007.[13] It is a slogan that means a multitude of things to many of its advocates – 'a conceptual fog', as the writer Aditya Chakrabortty puts it and a blank canvas onto which is projected hopes for a better environment, a fairer workplace and a more robust democracy. But at its heart, as he rightly acknowledges, it is a recognition that the future could – and should – look better than the past.[14]

Climate change requires an energy revolution that will transform Britain's post-industrial economy. As fossil fuels have been phased out, jobs have been painfully lost, but the battery, wind, solar, tidal and hydrogen that will power us through the future will create many more. The road to net zero is paved with a million climate jobs, many of them in research, design, engineering and manufacturing, should we choose to rise to the moment. Because of their location, assets and industrial legacy, communities that have been hardest hit by the loss of industry and the precarious gig economy jobs that have replaced it – from Yorkshire and the Humber to Fife and Aberdeenshire – are well placed to benefit. Grimsby, which is now home to a thriving wind industry, is on the exposed East coast of one of the windiest places in Europe, while Rotherham houses an advanced manufacturing hub in part because of the steel cutting skills which existed in the region and can be adapted to advanced manufacturing. The decision to subsidise households to install solar power was an environmental move but also one that, literally, shifted power to community energy cooperatives and small companies in every part of the UK, providing good employment opportunities everywhere.

The US Government has been among the first to realise this, introducing a game-changing $369bn subsidy to grow domestic energy production. The Inflation Reduction Act will create millions of well paid jobs in the parts of America that have been overlooked and ignored for so long.

But here in the UK the government has followed a very different path. In 2015 ministers effectively banned new onshore wind through changes to planning laws and cancelled planned investment in carbon capture and storage, and the Swansea Bay tidal lagoon. Then they cut subsidies to households who installed solar panels by 65 per cent, threatening thousands of jobs. Just a few weeks before I had been standing with young apprentices in Warrington who were proudly showing me the work they were doing on their own estate, cutting energy bills for residents, and thereby keeping badly needed money in the community, gaining new skills and protecting the planet. Their jobs meant everything to them, but their potential loss gained little traction in Parliament and barely featured in the public debate. While the hundreds of steel jobs which were under threat did (rightly) get much attention in that time, the thousands of jobs in solar energy did not. Solar was one of the fastest-growing sectors in the UK economy. Just a year later the solar industry reported that more than half of the 35,000 UK jobs had been lost.[15]

One reason for this disparity is effective campaigning by the major trade unions who represent steel workers. They worked tirelessly to keep the pressure up on government to intervene and it is testimony to their impact that they forced the threat to steel onto the political agenda, albeit with a muted response from government. But it was a reminder, too, that in the private sector, particularly where sectors like solar energy are dominated by small, diffuse employers, unions face greater barriers to the workplace, and people's ability to exercise a voice or a say is far, far weaker.

But could this be different? Britain's largest trade union, Unite, took on a bus company in Manchester, Go North West, which was trying to fire and rehire 500 drivers at the start of the pandemic.[16] They reached out to sympathetic politicians for support on the picket line and in Parliament, all traditional and often vital activities. But Unite's leverage team had also found out that the company was bidding for a multi-billion pound rail contract in Norway and reached out to sympathetic Norwegian politicians, alerting them to the bus company's tactics. Unite's general secretary told the *Guardian* newspaper, 'suddenly I was in the room with the CEO of the parent company and he signed a statement to say that they would not be using fire and rehire ... That stopped it for the sector. Other companies knew they could not get away with it.'[17]

This is just one of a few brilliant examples of how to do things differently in a modern landscape that we have largely so far failed to adapt to. If we got this right – working together, across local, regional and national boundaries – the possibilities that automation, education and the road to net zero have opened up should help people live larger, richer, more dignified lives with job opportunities, choices and chances that didn't exist before. And if unions can do it, why not governments?

RIGHTS

Sharon Graham is the first female general secretary of Unite and one of a number of women who have emerged at the forefront of the trade union movement in recent years. They include the fearless Mary Bousted of the National Education Union, Christina McAnea of UNISON, and the TUC's Frances O'Grady, who brokered the biggest labour market intervention in modern times – the furlough scheme – which was the only (brief) re-emergence of tripartism in the workplace since the 1970s.

The expansion of women into the workforce has been one of the most dramatic transformations of the past forty years. In 1979, just over half of working-age women were in employment. Today it's three-quarters.

In some arenas this was previously simply unthinkable. I served as shadow foreign secretary at a time when the world was still coming to terms with a generation of women diplomats who were smashing glass ceilings in key diplomatic postings. Until 1973, the Foreign Office, like many employers, operated a so-called 'marriage bar', which often called for the termination of the employment of a woman on her marriage, so for women it was work or family: you simply couldn't have both. Today's generation of inspiring diplomats is led by no-nonsense northerner Karen Pierce, who has made waves as the first female – and highly effective – ambassador to the United States. In my first Zoom meeting with her she switched happily between discussion of the many causes of noise in my house (a restless six-year-old and a lively VE day party held by my neighbours outside) to the challenges Putin and Xi Jinping posed to the West, and the causes of populism in the US and UK.

But while women have been able to break into some of the most powerful jobs in the world, so many of the jobs created from the 1980s onwards filled by women were private sector, part-time and low-paid, and opportunities for representation were few and far between. Although half of all union members are now women, three quarters of the female workforce aren't represented by a union at all.[18] Childcare was seen as a private, not public, concern until a generation of women MPs, like Tessa Jowell and Harriet Harman, forced it onto the political agenda, and even now, despite its centrality to the economy, it isn't treated as a major plank of national infrastructure. Their generation won the right to take on earning responsibilities while retaining the bulk of caring responsibilities.

In our house this wasn't the whole picture. My dad prided himself on 'doing his bit' around the house, although the mess he made in the kitchen when he made dinner was legendary. But in the later years, after they divorced, I grew up in a one-parent household at a time when 'single mums' were being vilified by our own Government and we felt the pressure to show we were just as good as anyone else. My mum was one of the first women to make it as a producer at Granada TV and ran a busy newsroom, often arriving home from work pretty exhausted but with plenty of time and energy for my sister and me. It was only later that I discovered that she would often return to work to edit programmes like World in Action late into the night, using a substantial part of her wages to pay for our amazing childminder.

There were some days when that just wasn't possible, one of which will stay with me forever: 15 April 1989. That afternoon news began to filter through that there was a major problem at the Hillsborough Stadium in Sheffield. As my mum directed the news, my sister and I sat in a corner of the newsroom at Granada watching the horrors unfolding on TV screens around us until, late into the night, mum bundled us into a taxi to stay the night at a friend's house. She ran that newsroom but I don't remember many other women being there, and I certainly don't remember anyone else juggling desperately important decisions – some of the footage they shot would later become critical in achieving justice for the 96 – alongside childcare responsibilities. They said women could have it all – they meant we could do it all.

Still now many of those women who are breaking glass ceilings in diplomacy recount compromises that sound far too familiar. One of them, Anne-Marie Slaughter, the first woman to serve as director of policy planning at the US State Department (one of the top foreign policy jobs in the world) wrote after leaving her job: 'I still strongly believe that women can "have it all" (and that men can too) ... But not today, not with the way America's economy and society are currently structured. My experiences over the past three years have forced me to confront a number of uncomfortable facts that need to be widely acknowledged – and quickly changed.'[19]

This is even more true for women in low-paid, insecure work. One of the first cases I ever dealt with as a newly elected MP was a group of women home-care workers who were battling for decent pay and conditions after being outsourced to a company who paid little, put staff onto shifts at less than a few hours' notice and refused to count travel time as work. One woman told me she had been told to come to work that day with just an hour's notice, and so had to take her two young children with her on the eight-hour shift, leaving them in the car while she went to care for people in their homes.

Rights of all kinds are slow to materialise, taking decades of campaigning and tireless work. By 1990, the country had had a woman prime minister for a decade but married women were still denied rights over their bodies and their finances: married women were still denied their own income tax return until 1990, while rape in marriage was still not recognised as a crime until the following year. Things have changed, but how far have we actually come? Still now, only 1 per cent of reported rape cases end in conviction[20] and violence against women and girls remains a scar on the nation. Despite the brilliance of the Equal Pay Acts (1963 and 1970), sixty years later three quarters of companies still pay men more than women for doing the same job. Shared parental leave was a landmark moment which allowed men to spend time with their children and gave women some flexibility and choice. But it has a take-up rate of only 2 per cent because men, who typically earn more, are less likely to be able to share the caring responsibilities. The advances won by the last generation have meant that a different kind of conversation is possible. The fact we haven't had it means that the promise to a generation of young women has not been met and economic and societal gains have not been felt equally. Too many people – not just women – are still held back and have fewer choices and chances because of who they are.

In the 1970s, my parents were looking for a house in the south Manchester suburb where I was born. When my mum turned up alone to see the estate agent there were plenty of houses to choose from but when my (Indian) dad appeared all the houses had mysteriously gone. I once asked my dad when he knew he wanted to leave academia to join the race relations struggle and he answered 'It wasn't a choice.' If he wanted to go for a drink with his wife, it took a sit-in to achieve it. When he applied for part-time work as a postman while studying at Leeds University he was turned down on the grounds of poor literacy – two years later he graduated with a double-starred first in English Literature. These were the experiences that led him and others to borrow techniques from the United States and pioneer them in Britain for the first time. One example was the blind job application, a social experiment where volunteers applied for jobs using identical CVs. Some had names on them that would be perceived to be 'white British' while others would use names that suggested the applicant was from a minority ethnic background. My dad's generation is often pessimistic about the impact they made – a repeat of this experiment in 2009 found minority applicants still had to send nearly twice as many applications to gain an interview as a white candidate[21] – but when I think about it, I think it is my generation who dropped the ball. For disabled people, women, mixed-race kids like me and the LGBTQ+ kids I grew up with, rights on paper have not translated to a society where we can walk the streets, travel on public transport or enter the workplace without adjusting our expectations.

Law usually responds to changes in public opinion but there have been moments when policymakers have tried to get out ahead of public opinion and use the law as a tool to change it. This was the brilliance of the 1976 Race Relations Act, introduced by Labour Home Secretary Roy Jenkins, which made it unlawful to discriminate on grounds of race, colour, nationality (including citizenship), and national or ethnic origin. It was rare and radical but never intended to be the final word, so it included provisions that established equality bodies like the Equal Opportunities Commission to carry the torch forwards.

The progress in the 1970s perhaps led many in my generation to believe that the arc of history always bends towards progress. But the struggle for equal rights is never won, the baton simply passed from one generation to the next.

When I look back on the time I spent at the Children's Society, battling for rights for refugee children as the head of our work with child refugees, my one regret is that too often we thought there were short cuts. The many things I was involved with were driven by the urgency of the situation – those children could not wait for change. So we took the last Labour Government to the Supreme Court to try to overturn laws that made migrant children destitute in the UK, and we helped win battles in the House of Lords, and eventually the House of Commons, to end the detention of children in the immigration system. But I wish I had spent more time and energy in the town hall meetings and community centres across Britain making the case directly to the public. Because, while politicians can sometimes get out ahead of public opinion and lead it, as Jenkins did, that change is so much more likely to come – and so much more likely to last – when the public support it. I was reminded of this as I struggled to convince a sceptical public of the case for remaining in the EU during the last referendum. Too many supporters of Britain's EU membership hadn't won – or even tried to make – the argument in recent years. It was a stark reminder that there are no shortcuts.

In the last few years the architecture of justice has also come under attack. Despite huge strides forward in legislation – the Race Relations Acts, Equal Pay Acts, the Human Rights

Act and Disability Discrimination Acts – big cuts to legal aid, employment tribunal fees and limits to judicial review have wiped out at a stroke hundreds of years of struggle to achieve them. What use are rights that cannot be realised? This matters to us all. The mark of a healthy democracy is surely the right to challenge. 'Sunlight,' as US Supreme Court Justice Louis Brandeis famously said, 'is the best disinfectant.' Something has gone very wrong when people cannot challenge the decisions of their own Government.

MAKING THE GRADE

In 1998 I set off for Newcastle University, a brilliant institution that until 1963 had been one of the many excellent Durham colleges, but not yet the world leading establishment it has since become in its own right. It was also one of the institutions at the forefront of an explosion of higher education across the country under Labour since 1997.

In 1999 the New Labour Government announced its ambition that 50 per cent of all young people would go on to university. When I was born only one in seven young people had that opportunity; by 2019 it was one in two, and the promise made two decades earlier had been realised.

New Labour's ambition was a central plank of the commitment to increase opportunities for young people from poorer backgrounds. On average, women who get to university earn a £100,000 earnings bonus over their lifetime, and men £130,000 – and they have far more choices than those who don't (although the research also finds one in five would have been better off not going at all).[22] But ministers believed it wasn't just central to individual success but central to the future of Britain. The argument, still made forcefully by Tony Blair, is that increasing the number of university graduates by only 1.5 per cent could boost GDP by the equivalent of more than £1,200 per person.[23] This was the central idea behind the New Labour Government. In a globalised world, equipping young people to compete was not just the right thing to do. It was the only thing to do. Yet, given this, a country known around the world for its universities is still found wanting in using one of its biggest exports to boost opportunity for young people in every part of Britain, and by extension for Britain as a whole.

While world-renowned universities, from Oxbridge to Leeds – whose leading literary professor, Arnold Kettle, was the draw that persuaded my dad to choose Britain in the 1950s – continue to attract more than half a million international students a year, the dream for too many here in Britain has not been realised. Whether or not you make it depends on who you are and where you live. Young people on free school meals are less than half as likely to go to university as their more affluent peers.[24] And while it's well known that relatively affluent, white young people from private schools are far more likely to get to Oxbridge, it is also true that nearly half of those admitted are from London and the South East. I see it in my own constituency where there is a newly built estate whose homes sell for way above local market rates and which attract young families who commute to higher-paid jobs in Manchester. Some 60 per cent of young people from that post-code go on to university, compared to a third for Wigan as a whole[25] – or to put it another way, if you live on that estate you're twice as likely to make the grade. Where you come from continues to determine how far you go.

THE MERITOCRACY MYTH

> 'I want Britain to be the world's great meritocracy – a
> country where everyone has a fair chance to go as far
> as their talent and their hard work will allow.'
>
> Theresa May, 2016

The advances of recent years have led us to believe anyone can have it all if only we try hard enough.

The goal of a true 'meritocracy' has been championed by politicians from Tony Blair to David Cameron, and from Theresa May to Boris Johnson. And who could disagree? Who would argue against a society where talent and effort alone are enough to carry you forwards towards the promise of a richer, larger, more secure life? And not just for you but for your children too. Most people would take that over a society where the circumstances of your birth determine how far you can go.

In his 1958 book, *The Rise of the Meritocracy*,[26] Michael Young described a society in which talent and effort, or 'merit' (IQ + effort = merit) was enough to succeed. The term he made famous – meritocracy – has since been used by politicians of all parties to describe the ideal society. But Young's book was a satire designed to demonstrate how a country in which advancement was dependent on birth, and hence blocked to so many, had given way to a society in which the chosen few, who met a narrow set of values, were given the seal of approval.

In this fictional future, advancement for the many remained closed – including those with acres of talent who were unable to meet the narrow tests set for them – while the idea that any of us could 'make it' freed the rich and powerful from any criticism. Years later, having watched much of what he predicted come to pass, and the pitfalls he warned of ignored, even championed, by successive governments, Young wrote: 'So assured have the elite become that there is almost no block on the rewards they arrogate to themselves. The old restraints of the business world have been lifted and, as the book also predicted, all manner of new ways for people to feather their own nests have been invented and exploited ... As a result, general inequality has been becoming more grievous with every year that passes.'

This is the theme taken up and expanded on by the philosopher Michael Sandel. In his 2020 book, *The Tyranny of Merit*,[27] he takes aim at what he calls the 'rhetoric of rising' – an article of faith for politicians of left and right alike. A belief that by levelling the playing field we ensure that those who rise to the 'top' deserve their success, while other blue-collar workers who are given the same chance to better their lot spurn it.

The argument has power, Sandel says, because 'it seems on the face of it to be empowering – we can make it on our own, we can make it if we try. It's a certain picture of freedom but it's flawed. It leads to a competitive market meritocracy that deepens divides and corrodes solidarity.'

Or, as the journalist Julian Coman puts it, they 'carry the burden of their own failure'.[28] Successive studies have shown that a belief in meritocracy is not only widespread and entrenched but that its corollary can be lower self-esteem, feelings of doubt and inadequacy, and even ill health linked to stress amongst those who are deemed to have failed 'the merit test'.

For years politicians have praised and championed the notion of a meritocracy, apparently unaware that it was a satirical warning – that merit could become just another way of keeping people down. But its champions insist that hard work and talent are what counts. Shall we see?

MONEY IS POWER

On 14 June 2017, in a flat in West London, an electrical fault with a fridge freezer would, within hours, spark one of the worst disasters of modern times. Grenfell Tower was a block covered in highly combustible cladding. Within minutes the fire had raced up the outside of the building and all four sides were alight. Two hours later and all twenty-three floors were ablaze. When the blackened building emerged from the smoke the full horror became clear: seventy-two people were dead and dozens more injured, among them young children, GCSE students, retired couples and entire families. As the family of seventy-eight-year-old Ligaya Moore poignantly put it, it was a tragedy that turned 'laughter into silence'.

How was such a tragedy possible in modern Britain? In the months that followed, as a public inquiry got underway, it would become clear that this was not the first fire in a block with similar cladding. We learnt that the Government was aware of problems as early as 1986 – well before a block of flats in Merseyside, North West England, caught alight in 1991. The fire at Knowsley Heights was followed by similar events spanning three decades, from Irvine in Scotland to Southwark in South London, in which six people lost their lives. In those intervening decades the alarm was raised many times. One parliamentary inquiry warned 'it should not take a serious fire in which many people are killed before all reasonable steps are taken towards minimising the risks'.[29] How did those warnings go unheeded?

The Government's lawyer told the official Grenfell Tower Inquiry, 'within the construction industry there was a race to the bottom, with profits being prioritised over safety'.[30] But who permitted it? Over thirty years and five different governments, how did it come to pass that profits were allowed to matter more than people, where the concerns and lives of people in the centre of one of the wealthiest boroughs in the wealthiest city in the country could be ignored – effectively rendered invisible to decision makers only a few miles away.

Six years after the Grenfell tragedy, on a hot summer's day, I walked again with the community on their annual silent march. As we approached the site of the tower, the procession slowed. People who had lost so much stopped to applaud the firefighters who had been there on the day and who come back to the spot to mark this moment every year since. As some of them told me later, they will be there for the community until justice is served and they are needed no more. But while the firefighters have been constant, six years after a tragedy that rocked a nation nobody has been held to account for Grenfell; nearly 40 per cent of buildings covered in similar cladding have not had it removed; and justice has not been done.

This is undeniable evidence of the unequal society we live in, where lives can be weighed against profit in a balance sheet and come out worse – where those who lack money also lack power and are not seen or heard.

WELCOME TO MODERN BRITAIN

Gross inequality is evident in Britain for anyone who cares to look for it – and it isn't because there isn't enough to go around. The UK has the fifth most unequal income distribution of the 19 OECD countries. As Torsten Bell of the Resolution Foundation explains, while 'typical households in the UK, France and Germany have remarkably similar incomes – around €34,000 in 2018 ... those similarities hide big differences. The rich here have incomes 17% higher than their equivalents in France, a kind of inequality many can live with. But no one should be happy with the fact that our poorest households have to survive on incomes a staggering 20% lower than those across the Channel.'[31]

Over my lifetime, inequality has grown. The share of income earned by the top 1 per cent in the UK has been rising since 1980, reaching its peak at a staggering 13 per cent in 2015, far higher than many comparable countries.[32]

Income and assets matter. They give people the resilience to survive shocks, without the grinding anxiety that comes with being only one payday away from disaster. A major global recession and an unprecedented global pandemic in the last decade have been brutal for many in Britain. On a visit to meet local firefighters I was stunned to hear how many now had second jobs, working at weekends and evenings when they weren't on the rota just to make ends meet. What is still considered a skilled, difficult and high-risk vocation now pays so poorly that firefighters are taking jobs as delivery drivers and in local takeaways just to take care of their families. I could see the stress and anxiety etched on their faces.

In modern Britain, wealth is even more unequally distributed than income, and as that wealth is passed down through generations the system replicates itself. Meritocracy is a con trick. The winners continue to win, the losers continue to lose.

In the years after the global financial crash, Prime Minister David Cameron and Chancellor George Osborne, launched a decade of harsh, deep cuts to public spending, arguing it was the only way to reset the economy. But, he declared, 'those with the broadest shoulders will bear the greatest burden'.

They didn't. A decade ago, the top 10 per cent of households owned 4.4 times as much as the bottom 50.[33] Today they own over five times (5.3) as much. The richest 10 per cent of households now hold 44 per cent of all wealth. The poorest 50 per cent, by contrast, own just 9 per cent. And once again it is not evenly distributed across the country. Households in the South East are twice as wealthy as households in the North West.

The richest now own 677 times more wealth than those at the very bottom. This is the highest wealth inequality on record. The belief that those who work hard and have talent do well is widespread in Britain. But those who lack money also lack power, and the consequences are corrosive.

THE POWER ELITE

In 2021 Greensill Capital collapsed, putting thousands of jobs at risk across Australia and the UK. One steel worker, who had worked at the plant for a decade, said: 'we don't know what else we would do'. In the inquiry that followed it emerged that Lex Greensill was given 'extraordinarily privileged' access to Downing Street because of lobbying by the former prime minister David Cameron, who texted and lobbied the chancellor and permanent secretaries across Whitehall on the company's behalf. While steel workers fought for their jobs, according to BBC's *Panorama*, David Cameron walked away with £7 million for his efforts.[34]

This grubby scandal shone a spotlight on a system which allows a chosen few with unparalleled access to power to milk the system until it breaks and a government that supports them. This is what C. Wright Mills called 'the power elite' in his 1970s book of the same name:[35] a revolving door between business, politics and media – the wealthy and powerful –

who rig the game for themselves. They can take risks happy in the knowledge that if they win, they win big, but if they lose, it is never them that bear the consequences. It's people like the steel workers of Rotherham and Hartlepool who will shoulder the appalling losses.

Our politics has failed when national governments do not back their own people.

THE POWER SHIFT

It is a source of concern to politicians of all parties that across the country foreign actors are buying up assets – football clubs are a prime example – that give them significant influence over democracy. In an unacceptable reminder of how close this gets, when the Saudi regime ran into difficulties buying Newcastle United in 2021, the Saudi crown prince, Mohammed bin Salman (who had recently been found to have ordered the murder of journalist Jamal Khashoggi) texted Boris Johnson that UK–Saudi Arabian relations would be damaged if the British Government failed to intervene to 'correct' the Premier League's 'wrong' decision not to allow a £300m takeover of Newcastle United.[36]

Dark money continues to flow into the City of London, sustaining authoritarian regimes overseas, including the Putin regime, which has interfered in British elections and used chemical weapons on the streets of the UK, murdering a British citizen. That same dark money often finds its way into housing, pushing up house prices and shutting out local people, constraining their choices and devaluing their worth.

My own council has followed the example of nearby councils and the city-region in handing out a contract for construction work in Wigan's town centre to a Chinese state-backed firm. British businesses who apply cannot compete with the power of the Chinese Government. There have been attempts to blame the councils involved, but there is a reason why more and more councils under all political leaderships are turning to China. Between 2010 and 2015, councils lost 27 per cent of their core spending power, weakening their options,[37] while Chinese companies are bolstered by the backing of the Chinese Government. This puts British businesses out of work, allows the Chinese Government to extend its influence across Britain, and opens up British democracy to manipulation. A few people win. The rest of us lose.

When power shifts away from the people in a democracy it is bound to trigger a reaction. In some parts of the UK this is precisely what has happened. As power has shifted to a privileged few, often overseas, and from nation states to powerful multinationals, it has opened up a democratic deficit, which is felt most acutely in some parts of Britain where communities have changed dramatically in recent decades. To understand it, you have to start with one of the biggest trends of recent decades: ageing.

GROWING OLDER ALONE

Our population is growing – but it is also ageing rapidly. There are now more over eighties, over nineties and older people generally than at any other point in human history. At a human level this is a profound achievement. There are more people than ever before who get to meet and bond with their own grandchildren, to live full lives after retirement, and to contribute decades of experience to their communities and to the country. But we have parked the question of how to fund the costs associated with an ageing society in the 'too difficult' box. Social care is at breaking point and the cost of pensions is rising, forcing an increase in the retirement age. Some countries have dealt with these challenges through taxation – sometimes fair, sometimes not – while others, like Germany, have sought to increase their working-age population through immigration. In Britain, governments have just ducked the challenge and by doing so have passed it on to people themselves.

Some places have felt this challenge more acutely because, as Ian Warren, who co-founded the Centre for Towns with me, has shown, the ageing population is now concentrated in particular parts of Britain. Unlike forty years ago, most older people are now in villages and towns, outside the big urban centres to which young people have to gravitate to find education, work and opportunity. These are the places where pressure on social care is most acute, and society is strained by a crisis of loneliness as people grow old hundreds of miles from children and grandchildren.

The political response to this has been largely to ignore it or, for lack of any real understanding, to make it far, far worse. To make badly needed savings in healthcare, many local and regional leaders, backed by government, have chosen to centralise services – not in the towns and villages where the need is greatest, but in the cities, leaving those who most frequently rely on healthcare having to travel the furthest to access it. The combination of ill health and poor public transport often means they are simply unable to do so. It is just one example of how the failure to look at the impact of decisions on entire places – to consider the geography of inequality – is felt as a tyranny in the places affected. Whole communities have been rendered invisible, with decisions made miles away by people with no stake in the outcome. It was little wonder that in 2019, when Boris Johnson promised to set this right by 'levelling up' the country, people responded. Three years later he left office, having presided over growing geographical inequality and a litany of broken promises. What little life there was in his agenda died with his departure.

THE TYRANNY OF THE MINORITY

Britain is, and remains, one of the most centralised countries in the world, with staggering levels of inequality between regions (one study concluded we are the most regionally unequal country in the developed world)[38] and within them. Only two regions do better than the national average – London and the South East – which by coincidence is where power lies. This is where most senior politicians of all political parties live – using schools, healthcare and public transport, and travelling to their constituencies only at weekends. Some 68 per cent of senior civil servants in the UK are based in London, including most of the team tasked with levelling us up.[39]

A staggering six of the eight commissioners on the National Infrastructure Commission, which recommends which major projects should be funded, are London-based and London specialists.[40] Little wonder then that infrastructure spending is dominated by London and the South East, with a plethora of massive infrastructure projects rolled out in the capital in the last two decades. They make investment decisions on the basis of where best to boost productivity. This is how investment continues to be funnelled into parts of the country that are already doing well. As they pull further and further ahead, others fall further behind.

Even on a generous estimate, the Government spends seven times as much on transport for every person in London as in the North East of England, a region that is crying out for better infrastructure.[41] In Blackhalls, County Durham, the community lost all seven stations under the Beeching rail reforms in the 1960s and has never regained them. Across Sunderland, County Durham and Northumberland, people are cut off from access to essential services – to the job centres that help them to survive and the A&E services that keep them alive – for lack of decent buses, trains and train stations. Little wonder there is anger at remote decision makers who continue to pile investment into their own city nearly 300 miles away.

The disconnect is staggering. London and the South East is the only part of the UK where people rely more on rail than buses. There are 2.5 times more bus journeys than train journeys every year, almost exactly the proportion by which trains dominate the political debate. Trains were discussed twice as often in the House of Commons in the last session of Parliament as buses. When the then Labour Leader, Jeremy Corbyn, raised the decimation of the bus network at Prime Minister's Questions he was mocked and ridiculed by political commentators. 'Jesus wept,' wrote one commentator. 'Is it transport questions or PMQs?' wrote another.

But without the buses and trains to carry people to work, without the rail and motorway networks to transport goods, and without the broadband and investment in the skills of the young people who grow up in those places, businesses do not invest and too often the story is of a spiral of decline where young people have to get out to get on. Another study by the Centre for Towns and Ernst & Young found that foreign direct investment to core cities has increased four-fold since 1997, while foreign direct investment to towns – small to begin with – stayed flat.[42] In 2019, 59 per cent of all foreign direct investment coming into the UK went to the core cities of London, Manchester, Leeds, Sheffield, Nottingham, Bristol, Cardiff, Liverpool, Glasgow, Edinburgh and Birmingham.

Half went to London. And in 2023 the same survey found that of all the steps the UK could take to improve its attractiveness to investors, geographical rebalancing of the UK economy was by far the most cited (by 30.3 per cent of those surveyed).[43]

This is important because a focus on 'regional' inequality ignores the huge disparities within those regions. For many people in remote parts of Wales, the North, the Midlands, Scotland or the South, those cities – Cardiff, Glasgow, Manchester and Birmingham – are as distant as Westminster.

Even the winners are losing. This is what forces young people to pile into major cities seeking work and opportunity, pushing up house prices, creating air pollution and straining public services in those places. A few years ago, I went to speak to national business leaders at a conference in Salford's MediaCity about the work we had done on this at the Centre for Towns, and I was approached at the end by an executive in one of the world's biggest social media companies. He described what this meant to him, since he was unable to move back home, his mum was growing older, increasingly in need of care, while he and his young family lived hundreds of miles away. His brother had remained at home and had a low-paid job with little chance of progression. Their friends, views and lives had grown apart as their experiences had followed different paths. Of course not everyone chooses to stay, or to return home. But that should be their choice, not ours. By taking away those choices from people, with only a handful of exceptions, everybody loses.

DEVOLUTION

Devolution was supposed to put this right. When Tony Blair announced that Labour would create a Scottish Parliament – ahead of the landslide 1997 general election – he said it would 'show the whole of the UK that there is a better way that Britain can be governed, that we can bring power closer to the people, closer to the people's priorities and that we can give Scotland the ability to be a proud nation within the United Kingdom'.[44]

Rhodri Morgan inspired people to believe in devolution because, he said, we have 'a vision of devolution and democratic politics that involves people in the democratic process of rebuilding the bond between politicians of all parties – in particular my own – and the people of Wales'.[45]

In 1999, the first secretary of Wales, Ron Davies, memorably described devolution as a process, not an event, 'and neither is it a journey with a fixed end-point. The devolution process is enabling us to make our own decisions and set our own priorities, that is the important point. We test our constitution with experience and we do that in a pragmatic and not an ideologically driven way.'[46]

These were powerful principles that were to lead to significant reforms but in later years, under successor governments, the agenda began to drift. Twenty years later, with support for independence in Wales and Scotland standing at 30–40 per cent and 40–50 per cent respectively, the bonds that hold the UK together are undeniably fraying.

The creation of devolved governments in Wales and Scotland was followed decades later by the Conservative chancellor George Osborne's introduction of city-region mayoralties across England. It has resulted in a patchwork of devolution deals for some major cities and their surrounding areas, none of them determined by the people who live in them, and each with limited powers and resources, which continue to be decided by Whitehall and Westminster. Unlike New Labour's devolution proposals, which were put to the people of Scotland and Wales in a referendum, in this case democracy was an afterthought from the outset. A central government consultation to consider the impact of the first devolution deal in Greater Manchester ran for just three weeks, wasn't advertised and had only twelve responses, ten of them from the same council leaders who agreed to the deal in the first place.

Concerns were raised – and ignored – that it would suck up power, taking decisions from a local to a regional level, where direct accountability is much weaker, and enable the centre to hold their hands up when problems arise and say 'it is not my problem' – the exact words used by Deputy Prime Minister Nick Clegg, when I asked why a deal that was supposed to empower the people had cut them out altogether.[47]

There is still an obvious reluctance on the part of central government to trust local and regional leaders, which has resulted, in many cases, in city-regions hoovering up power from surrounding towns to try to deliver much-needed change, instead of being able to draw on powers cascaded down from Westminster. Hundreds of places across England that aren't near a major city have been shut out from power altogether. So it remains the case that remote politicians and civil servants sit at desks drawing lines on a map, and cancelling bus and train routes, which at one stroke cut young people off from apprenticeships, children from grandparents, parents from getting home on time to read their children a bedtime story. While people can rail against the system, they cannot change it.

It is a democratic deficit that has been felt acutely in Scotland for some time. But now in every nation and region of the UK there are those who feel it too.

A BETTER DEMOCRATIC SETTLEMENT

Britain, a country that once was emulated across the world for its model of democracy, is failing at its own game. As we struggle to define who we are in the world after leaving one of the world's biggest trading blocs, our democracy and our values should be our best export. Instead, we are in crisis. For all the lip service paid to moving power closer to the people, it remains too remote and too unaccountable to too many.

Take broadcasting, an absolutely critical industry, once described by the Annan Commission, which set up Channel 4, as 'the way a society talks about itself'. This matters in any society in which people can be considered to have a stake. And yet 88 per cent of broadcast media jobs are in London and the South East, shutting out much of Britain from the national conversation. Welcome attempts in recent years to address this have resulted in major media organisations,from the BBC to Channel 4, moving staff North – important and right in its intentions. But Channel 4 is the organisation that has notably moved not just its programming, but its commissioners, who decide what is made and what is seen and which of us are reflected in our own national story.

Dorothy Byrne, its first female editor of news and then editor at large, broke many taboos taking on the dominance of male Oxbridge graduates in the media and the macho culture that so often prevails.

I know her best as the energetic, fun woman who came to stay with us in our south Manchester semi in the 1990s. Unbeknownst to me and my sister she was already becoming one of the foremost journalists of her generation and a fellow kindred spirit with my mum in what looked very much like a man's world. Delivering the McTaggart Lecture decades later she (half) joked: 'I've been temporarily kidnapped, condemned as a terrorist whore, told by my own colleagues I should be imprisoned for several years and hardest of all been a single parent ... I started out in television at Granada and from my very first day the overwhelmingly male management made me feel at home. Or to be more accurate, they tried to come home with me.'[48]

Perhaps it's because of the battles she has had to fight that she is one of the few voices asking, 'Where are the programmes which shake all our assumptions about society? ... When you change who is making TV, you change TV.'

I believe people in every part of Britain have something to offer and when we open up the conversation so that more of us can contribute, we all gain. It's the opposite of the approach the Johnson government made when it unveiled the centre-piece of its plan to 'level up' Britain: moving 500 treasury jobs to Darlington and 20 National Infrastructure Commission jobs to Leeds. Darlington is the North Eastern town that gave the world the first passenger steam railway, an engineering company that built bridges across the world from Sydney to the Humber, and can lay claim to our country's first national newspaper. It once stood at the centre of the world. Where is the assessment of the assets and potential in Darlington? Where is the investment in skills so that jobs created there are within reach of young people? And where is the plan for future industry, work and contribution that matches that proud history? If you ask local leaders they will tell you, but the people who make the decisions – the ministers and permanent secretaries – remain in central London, drawn from a narrow demographic pool with largely uniform backgrounds and experiences. Moving power is what counts.

I served as shadow energy secretary in 2015: a time of crisis for North Sea oil and gas. In just one year alone, the industry body revealed that 65,000 jobs had been lost. We worked hard with Aberdeen's city region to build a new research hub in wind energy, to which Aberdeen was uniquely well suited, as part of a plan to retrain and retain the skilled workforce. But I was curious to understand why every time we met it was in London, not Aberdeen. The answer was that the powers and funding they needed lay in the hands of a junior minister in Whitehall – who almost always had dozens of more pressing things to attend to than the future prospects of thousands of people at the other end of the UK.

Our democratic institutions are unfit for the promise of our age. Power is held by too few people in too few places and the contribution most of us have to make has been written off and written out of our national story. Our electoral system encourages conflict where cooperation is needed, erases complexity and difference and shuts out minority views from finding expression – what Alexis De Tocqueville identified, centuries ago, as the tyranny of the majority. The sharp limitations of referendums have been exposed in recent years, in Scotland and then again across the UK, exposing and encouraging divisions rather than enabling reconciliation. Even locally it is hard to hold power to account. There are too few levers. People often lack basic information about decisions made on their behalf. When the vast majority of local councillors represent only one party, whichever party it happens to be, it is too easy for a culture to grow up that is resistant to challenge.

But at home and abroad there are clues to a better future. My own council, responding to looming austerity, decided to make a covenant with the people of Wigan. The Wigan Deal was based on a recognition that Wigan would not survive cuts of 50 per cent to the council's budget without the consent, support and creativity of all of its residents.

Inspirational chief executive Donna Hall led discussions in the community centres, sports venues, pubs and town halls across the borough, and the Deal was born. The council dropped plans to close libraries in former pit villages – where our very youngest and oldest residents lived, bus services were scarce and libraries were a lifeline. In return, the people stepped up, taking over those libraries as volunteers or in partnership with charities. The Beech Hill library run by volunteers with the charity Bookcycle is now better used than it was before austerity hit.

In Ireland, citizens' assemblies have shown how the most contentious, emotional issues can find resolution when the people are brought into the conversation. Just like the hospital workers in Wigan, people want to be part of the democratic process and they should be trusted to participate. Other countries have seen their democracies strengthened by involving the public alongside parliamentarians in meaningful decision making. It hasn't just been in Ireland, where decades of deadlock on abortion and same-sex marriage gave way to a new consensus. It has also happened in Iceland (after the banking crisis), and in Canada and Australia, through assemblies on issues like nuclear waste and constitutional reform, have shown dialogue can produce lasting change.

Like a circuit-breaker, citizens' assemblies can disrupt bad habits: kicking issues into the long grass, placing party interests over the national interest and assuming the public are unable to cope with hard choices. By bringing the people back into the conversation, Parliaments have been able to reject binary choices, allowing randomly selected groups of citizens to explore options in an open forum and make recommendations to elected MPs, who retain the final say. When a cross-party group of MPs – Stella Creasy, Caroline Lucas, Jo Swinson and I – called for a citizens' assembly to break the

Brexit deadlock, some MPs dismissively claimed we were asking people to do Parliament's job for us. But involving citizens in discussions doesn't diminish politics or politicians – it enhances the value of the conversation for both. Throughout history, politics has had to find a path through huge and fundamental disagreements. As President John F. Kennedy wrote in *Profiles in Courage*, it very rarely happens that 'all the truth, and all the right, and all the angels are on one side'.[49] Letting a little light in is surely the way to build decisions that can last.

OUR NATIONAL STORY

During my lifetime, Britain has transformed and for a time it felt for many of my generation that the arc was bending towards progress. Thanks to advances in science and health-care we are living longer, healthier lives. With automation and a shift to net zero, so much of the backbreaking work in the mines, on the railways and in the forges has been replaced by service and white-collar jobs that should, in theory, offer the prospect of good wages, a contribution, and a longer, happier life. A generation of young people have been able to grasp hold of a future that was unimaginable to their grandparents and make it to university in record numbers. Women have been among the biggest beneficiaries of the expansion of education, and doors to the workplace that were previously closed have opened. The Equal Pay Act, the realisation of equal marriage, and the Race Relations Acts – the second of which was co-authored by my dad just years before I was born – allowed some of my generation, including me, to grow up with choices that were unthinkable to our parents.

But the local, national and international political systems we have built have created winners and losers: at times failing to keep pace with the new realities confronting us; at others, hijacked by a few for their own gain, leaving millions facing a very different reality than the future that should have been on offer. The pandemic brutally exposed two countries within one, each with very different experiences and choices on offer. The closer I look, the more I see that the creation of 'winners' and 'losers' is a result of who decides. When a few people in a few places dominate decision making, this shuts out the light and denies the whole country the chance to succeed. As we turn to face the future, the battery of challenges we face could be met by a country that was clear about what we could achieve and had a plan to match, with the foresight to put our people at its centre.

WHO IN THE WORLD ARE WE?

Britain stands outside of the EU for the first time in nearly half a century, and the ties that bind the UK together are fraying. For six years we spent so much time arguing about the present that we failed to think about the future. In the years since, the country has been through a pandemic led by a prime minister who presided over successive scandals, leaving office – and later Parliament – with trust in politics at an all-time low, followed by another who gambled Britain's security on big tax cuts for the wealthy, crashed the economy and left people paying the price through higher mortgages and rents for years to come. This, more than ever, is the moment to re-evaluate the country we are and the role we want to play in the world.

There are powers and funding that we had agreed to share with other European countries – pooling our sovereignty in pursuit of greater power – that will now be repatriated to Britain. Where such power and resources go will determine what we can do, who benefits, and whether we pull together or break apart.

But there is a deeper question about the country we want to be. Churchill famously defined three majestic circles through which Britain exerted influence: the Empire and Commonwealth, the United States and Europe. This is the story parts of the right nostalgically reach back to for a story about modern Britain – a country that punches above its weight, a small island that once ruled the waves and could again, never quite explaining how. Nostalgia has come to characterise much of the left too, conjuring up images of bygone days of men in tight-knit communities who heroically endured poverty while others were shut out from power. As the Sunderland MP Bridget Phillipson puts it, 'those who romanticise that past are seldom those who grew up in it'.

But countries that succeed are countries that know who they are and where they are going. Britain, by contrast, has something of an identity crisis. We are led by a government mired in sleaze, fresh out of energy and ideas. We have spent much of the last decade embroiled in angry debates about the future of the UK and our membership of the EU. From those debates surfaced something profound, about people's search for identity and belonging – the terms 'Leaver' and 'Remainer' becoming labels people willingly attached to themselves, dividing us from one another. But what of the common ground on which the future will be built?

There is, as Danny Boyle once said, darkness and light in our history. A self-confident country is one that can see this, learn from its past – good and bad – and look to the future with confidence and energy.

Ours is a country that once exported a model of representative democracy to the world. The Good Friday Agreement is still held up as an example of effective peace-building in conflict zones the world over. Our universities are among the best in the world and English amongst the most widely spoken languages. We have built one of the most comprehensive healthcare systems. At a time when climate change barely featured on the agenda, we gave the world the first ever Climate Change Act. And during the pandemic we showed how we cannot just lead but shape the world and the choices on offer to us, through science and research – finding a vaccine in record time, developing diagnostics and therapeutic treatment, and sharing the gene sequencing expertise that helped to identify new strains of the virus as they emerged.

Imagine if we became a country that threw those opportunities wide open. Imagine what we could do if democracy and human flourishing, social and environmental justice, scientific and educational advancement were the floodlights that lit our path at home and the flashlights overseas.

We could build an agenda for Britain that matches the ambition of the people in it – big and generous, not small and petty – measured not in the number of our flags but in the health of our children, the strength of our communities, the dignity of our workforce and the security of our nation. We could reset the approach of the last forty years and take long-overdue action to rebuild the economic security of Britain's people and the places we call home. We could make environmental security our priority, recognising that climate change threatens the future of our planet and the lives and prosperity of working-class people across our country and the wider world right now. It is a central pursuit of social justice, not an addition to it.

Those hospital workers in Wigan, that great untapped asset sitting right in front of us, point towards a different future: a country at ease with itself, that knows what it is for, that can deliver on our values at home and have the confidence to stand for them overseas. That country is at our fingertips. It is a country I have believed in all my life but have never yet seen. The time to build it is long overdue.

5.

THE ROAD
TO POWER

'The circumstances of our lives made it a burning,
luminous mark of interrogation. Where was power and
which the road to it?'

Aneurin Bevan

In 2021, with inflation rising, supermarket shelves lying
empty and the number of working people in poverty at a
record high, the *New Statesman* magazine declared: 'Britain
isn't working.'[1]

By the following summer this was no longer contested. The
Conservative Party leadership contender Rishi Sunak, who
had served, until just a few weeks before, as the chancellor of
the exchequer, declared the state of the economy a 'national
emergency'. Just months later the newly installed Prime
Minister Liz Truss resigned, only a few weeks into the job,
following a disastrous 'mini-budget' which sent the pound
into freefall and mortgage payments soaring. While they took
us from one crisis to another, there was so little space to
consider how we ended up here.

Much ink has been spilt trying to find the solution to
Britain's problems but the answer is simple. Hand people
power and resources and they will build a country that works.

After the EU Referendum, and out of frustration at the characterisation of majority Leave-voting places as 'left-behind wastelands', some friends and I set up an organisation called the Centre for Towns to bring people in those places back into the conversation. While newspaper columnists, politicians and assorted commentators scrambled to explain why it was that few of them had seen Brexit coming, many of those who had voted for it found the debate was taking place largely without them. When we asked people in Britain's towns what they wanted to fix, we expected them to say 'Brexit', but everywhere we went the two things that came up were transport and culture. Brexit barely featured.

The transport conversation normally began with traffic, potholes, buses or trains, but it didn't end there. We met young people who couldn't afford to take up apprenticeships because of the cost of travel; a girl who had spent her childhood in and out of care homes who could no longer see her nan – the one relationship that sustained her – because of a cancelled bus route; a dad who hadn't made it home on time to say goodnight to his kids for two years because of rail chaos in the North; and a pensioner who regularly spent five or six hours travelling twenty-eight miles to have cancer treatment because the services had been 'centralised' and the only passenger transport available had to pick up people across the region.

We hadn't ever expected arts and culture to matter so much – more than high streets, housing and education, which also featured – but once people began to talk it made complete sense. They no longer saw themselves or their communities reflected in the national story. Arts funding had retreated to cities that, for lack of transport and connection, most people were unable to access or shape. When funding was provided, decisions were made by funding bodies in London with limited understanding about what worked or what mattered to the local area and little idea about the history which underpinned the pride, identity and purpose of the area.

While reports are being written in the capital about 'engaging' people in arts and culture, people across Britain are clamouring for its return. Around that time, Maxine Peake was in a play called *Queens of the Coal Age* at Manchester's Royal Exchange, which told the story of the Women Against Pit Closures movement, whose grit and resolve kept the miners' strike alive. Some of the women who lived that struggle were in my constituency, but now, well into their retirement, to get back to Wigan after the play finished without a car was too difficult for them on public transport. So on one of our biggest estates they hired a minibus and went off to see themselves and their story reflected for the first time in a tale that had been told so often without them in it.

The conversation we started with people across Britain convinced me that not only were a group of decision makers based hundreds of miles away often the last to understand what was going wrong or how to fix it, but that we were having the wrong conversation – and worse, it was on their terms, not ours. Whether it was London, Brussels, Holyrood or the Senedd, decisions that were handed down from on high often missed the point completely, valuing the wrong things – two entirely separate conversations. I have come to see that this is the root of so much I have heard and felt across Britain: the feeling that modern politics is basically meaningless.

If people had their way, we would protect the things they value. Jobs that give young people the chance to grow and contribute to their communities and their country. The digital and transport infrastructure that connects us to each other and allows investment to flow. Healthcare that supports people to live the lives they want, close to home where they need it. The high streets, pubs and Post Offices that sustain community life; clean air and green spaces. Education that enables people to have choices, and live richer lives, where and when they need to, without dividing us arbitrarily into success and failure, winners and losers. Arts and culture that reflect us all in our national story. Isn't this the basis of a thriving country, one in which people genuinely have a say, chances and choices, one that can unlock the creativity and energy of its people, and live its values at home in order to stand for them abroad?

The pandemic confirmed that Labour's default (state intervention) and the Tories' default (to reach for the 'invisible hand' of the market) are each insufficient to confront the challenges we face.

In one of the most centralised countries in the world, the national state was unable to respond at speed to procure protective equipment for frontline workers and roll out the test and trace system during the COVID-19 pandemic, held back by lack of knowledge, too little flexibility and an inability to mobilise quickly.

Meanwhile, the Tory chancellor, one of the chief defenders of Britain's forty-year legacy of unrestrained, unregulated markets, had to abandon the idea that the market would provide and instead instigate a furlough scheme to prevent millions from losing their jobs and their income. It highlighted how our models of governance were built for an era with an industrialised economy – before mass education, before globalisation, and blind to the ways in which both states and markets can monopolise power and deny it to the people.

Security, choices and respect – this is what they ask and what will never be delivered by people with no stake in the outcome. Power has to return to the people.

You may be thinking this sounds a little like David Cameron's 'Big Society' – an insightful set of ideas about the importance of civic life which collapsed during the Coalition years into an agenda for shrinking the state and unleashing market forces. It isn't.

At the core of what I'm proposing is the belief that national government matters and has a role to play, both to provide the 'visible hand' that ensures private interests support the common good and to prevent money and power from being appropriated by any one group or entity. This is a critical job that in reality it has not been doing for decades. In the argument that has raged about state versus market, something has been lost – in the hurry to draw the battle lines, neither side paused to think through what states and markets can and should actually do for us.

The temptation in a book like this would be to set out a 'blueprint for Britain'. I should at this stage be about to launch into the five, ten, twenty things that would fix Britain and tell you how to change the world. Sorry to disappoint, but if you've got this far and think that's what I'm about to do, you have completely missed the point. The assumption that one person can hold all the answers, for all people, everywhere, is arrogant. It is what got us into this mess. The answers lie in people and communities and they must write the story of our future.

So in the pages that follow I am going to describe how they are starting to do that, and how some national governments have responded. It's here that we might find the seeds of change that show how Britain could be stronger, fairer, kinder and more secure. When things are fundamentally broken, some people give up and others rail against the system. This, though, is the story of those who have sought to change it. It shows us what the future could be if we reset the way we thought about politics, recognising that all of us have something to offer and something to learn.

The status quo is no alternative at all. Not just because our economic and political model doesn't work for most of us, but because people will no longer put up with it. The waves of populism, nationalism and political upheaval that have engulfed us are a roar of noise from people who have learnt that silent pain evokes no response. They demand a response. That is why we should seek power for one overriding purpose – to give it back.

'It was no abstract question for us,' said Nye Bevan, recalling his days as a South Wales miner. 'The circumstances of our lives made it a burning, luminous mark of interrogation.' The only question that mattered was 'where was power and which the road to it?'

THE FORK IN THE ROAD

Kicking off his US presidential campaign in 1968, Bobby Kennedy railed against the material poverty that scarred the nation and the poverty of ambition that scarred its leaders. 'When our forebears – yours and mine – came to America,' he said, 'they came because this country promised them something. It promised them an opportunity, nourished by education, not merely to grind for a bare living, but to strive for a good life.'[2]

Realising this promise in Britain today is both a moral imperative and a national emergency. Too much wealth is in too few hands, sucking the life from our towns and villages, stashed in offshore accounts instead of put to productive use – a system that favours those who extract over those who invest.

The challenge is how to make our economy work for most people to meet the challenges of this century and rebuild the country. Britons want and deserve the foundations of a good life, the ability to contribute to the future of their nation, and a share in its success. But somewhere along the way, political economy has become detached from people and their central concerns; our institutions have prevented things from changing; and we serve the economy, rather than it serving us. During my lifetime this has been treated by many politicians as entirely natural. But it was never inevitable.

Adam Smith is often called the father of modern economics, introducing concepts like GDP and many of the features of modern capitalism. He argued that people are rationally motivated and when they act with the aim of maximising their self-interest in pursuit of their individual goals an 'invisible hand' reconciles this multiplicity of (incompatible) goals to produce an orderly society.

In recent years – with the exception of the short-lived tenure of Liz Truss – I think David Cameron is the prime minister who most vigorously promoted the ideas that flow from this – arguing that unrestrained free markets allow the economy to grow and people to flourish. Cameron promised to build a land of opportunity by unleashing the 'wealth creators' and removing the obstacles that held them back: 'Profit, wealth creation, tax cuts, enterprise are not dirty, elitist words. They're not the problem, they really are the solution. Because it's not government that creates jobs, it's businesses. It's businesses that get wages into people's pockets, food on their tables, hope for their families and success for our country. There is no shortcut to a land of opportunity.'[3]

Cameron's vision, which borrowed heavily from Smith's belief in the efficiency of markets and the power of self-interest, was combined with austerity, a 'bonfire of the quangos' (quasi-autonomous non-governmental organisations) and the 'red tape challenge' that cut back oversight, spending and regulation. In short, a diminished, neutered state.

He really seemed to believe this would hold the answers. In 2007, as opposition leader, he said: 'when I say that we can make British poverty history please do not tell me that it cannot be done. Do not tell me that a society which can decode the human genome, build the world's greatest financial centre and provide the young men and women that form the finest armed forces on earth, cannot fight and win the battle against poverty.'[4] His time in office was characterised by sweeping cuts to universal credit and child benefits. By the time he left office, child poverty was projected to rise by over 50%, undoing all of the gains made since 1997.[5]

This approach was a grotesque distortion of the system Adam Smith proposed and the beliefs that underpinned it. Smith was not purely an economist, he was a moral philosopher who believed the economy was just one part of the human condition. His account of human nature in his 1759 book, *The Theory of Moral Sentiments*, clearly rejects the egoism that is often wrongly ascribed to him: 'How selfish soever man may be supposed, there are evidently some principles in his nature, which interest him in the fortune of others, and render their happiness necessary to him, though he derives nothing from it.'

His account of the economy is based on more than self-interest, describing a just society that was concerned about the welfare and prospects of its least well-off members, not just about economic success. He believed the invisible hand of the market could steer us towards a healthier, thriving economy *only* if the 'visible hand' of the state steered, mitigated and regulated excesses of the type that now characterise our modern economy.

Alongside philosopher David Hume, another giant of the

Scottish Enlightenment, he argued that social bonds and moral values are the foundation of political economy and that we should shape and build our economic institutions to foster them. Hume believed that allowing money to define our relationships – allowing 'cash' to become 'the sole nexus of man to man', as Thomas Carlyle put it – corrupts, distorts and diminishes society. And society matters – it is where the bonds that hold us together are forged. Enabling humans to prosper, to allow for the creativity and collective action that could be the building blocks of a modern, thriving economy – all of this rests on the pursuit of more than just self-interest.

How far from this we have travelled, invoking the names of those who held different values and envisaged an entirely different system. It is time to revive the goals of human advancement, security and stability that have been subsumed to profit. The democratic governments that have stepped out of the way as modern corporations have grown more powerful, wielding greater influence than many nation states, must step forward again. Money, ownership and power that is held by a few must be harnessed and mobilised again for the common good, not just private gain.

It is not just that too many people lose in the system we have. It is that those who lose simply cannot win. In his 1981 book, *Spheres of Justice*, the philosopher Michael Walzer showed how people who have money can use it to acquire and hoard power in other areas of life.[6] Appropriating wealth allows you to buy a better education, opening up the prospect of acquiring political power, and those who hold political power have greater access to money and education. It is, he argued, fundamentally unjust to allow this system to persist. 'Money', Walzer wrote, 'should be harmless.' His belief that holding power in one sphere should not allow someone to hold it in another was best summed up by his statement, 'good fences make just societies'. He is not alone in grappling with the yawning democratic deficit in our economy. The philosopher Michael Sandel, for example, has suggested that the absence of limits on what money can buy – university education, medical care, access to justice, political influence – has turned a market economy into a market society, allowing money to do great harm.

But for the most part this philosophical debate has barely permeated our politics. We have railed at the individuals who milk the system and asked how we can create a more diverse, elite group to make decisions on our behalf instead of focusing our energies on breaking open those spaces, to scatter and disperse economic and political power and restore it to those who rightfully own it. This failure to acknowledge the systemic nature of the problem is what, I think, accounts for the basic irrelevance of modern politics.

I wonder what Adam Smith, whose definition of a 'free' market was one that rejected monopolies and dispersed power, would make of a modern Tory Party that defends the concentration of power and the interests of organisations that are 'too big to fail'? Even the former Conservative adviser Nick Timothy decries 'capitalism in crisis.' 'We have built an economic model,' he writes 'that rewards the wealthy not the many, the bureaucrat not the entrepreneur, the rentier not the risk taker, the financier not the maker and the old not the young.'[7]

I still find it difficult to understand how the Liberal Democrats couldn't see that Brexit was driven in part by a modern society that denies millions of people the right to make meaningful choices about the things that matter. They believed that this act, born out of the tradition of John Stuart Mill, who recognised that the capacity to choose is what makes us human, was instead simply 'driven by nostalgia' for a time when 'passports were blue, faces were white and the map was coloured imperial pink'.

I believe my own party, Labour, also lost sight of an important part of our own tradition when in government: the belief that politics is not just about redistribution but about power. Trickle down redistribution that took a proportion of wealth from the top and handed it, with conditions, to those deemed worthy at the bottom was coupled with a trickle-out economics that moved investment and decision making to some parts of the country, mainly cities, in the hope that the benefits would be felt elsewhere. The reasons for this varied. For some it was born of necessity after eighteen years of Tory government left an urgent need to rebuild; for others it was always intended to be the first step on a road to more radical reform; and some thought it was a deliberate choice to take a new 'modernising' approach in contrast to the ideology of the 1970s. Whatever the motivation, it was an approach that, for all the good it did for the beneficiaries, left the existing power structures largely undisturbed.

'Socialists', wrote Clement Attlee, 'are not concerned solely with material things. They do not think of human beings as a herd to be fed and watered and kept in security. They think of them as individuals cooperating together to make a fine collective life. For this reason socialism is a more exacting creed than that of its competitors. It does not demand submission and acquiescence, but active and constant participation in common activities.'

This tradition has been lost to the paternalism and technocratic approach that came to characterise our recent past. Labour has always believed that by the strength of our common endeavour we achieve more than we achieve alone. Sharing power was once a core part of our history. It is central to our future.

THE NATIONAL CONTRIBUTION

This is not just a moral argument but an economic one too. A country that writes off people and assets from most of Britain cannot succeed. But Britain is now unique: a major country that believes it can power a modern economy using only a handful of people, in a handful of sectors, in one small corner of the country.

For nineteen of the last twenty years, only two regions, London and the South East, have had the backing and investment to make a net contribution to the UK economy, raising more in revenue than they received.[8] This has deep roots. Estimates of regional GDP per head from a century ago expose the same trend.[9]

It has left Britain overly reliant on the City of London, creating a lack of resilience that was only too apparent during the 2008 global financial crash. Our core cities have the lowest productivity of any large OECD country, performing at just 86 per of the UK average. Meanwhile many towns and villages have been written off altogether and the gap is growing. Even in the part of the North West where devolution is most advanced, the gap between the city of Manchester and the surrounding towns is large and has grown over the twenty-year period up to 2016 the city of Manchester's economy grew by 83 per cent while neighbouring Tameside grew by just 8 per cent.[10]

The fact that the United Kingdom is one of the most geographically unequal countries in the world is no longer a regional problem: it's a national problem. It has left us with the widest productivity gap in the G7, costing the UK economy an estimated £50 billion a year.[11]

Even the winners are losing. Nearly a million people make their home in London every year, seeking higher wages and better opportunities. Often, they find them. People in the London region have the highest disposable incomes by a long way. But that's only before housing costs are taken into account. Then, living standards fall way below much of the rest of the country.[12]

With inflation soaring, it is now widely accepted that growth is the only way out of our current crisis. We need all people in every place to be able to make a contribution again.

Markets alone will not deliver this; it will take the visible hand of the state. This is how the regional development agencies established by the last Labour Government were instrumental in bringing advanced manufacturing to Rotherham and wind energy to Grimsby. They saw the potential and built both the infrastructure – the roads, business parks, skills investment – and the partnerships, with universities and business, to ensure it succeeded.

This is the approach being taken by the German Government, led by Olaf Scholz, working in partnership with firms and workers to bring jobs to Eastern Germany that build on the skills that already exist there. In regions like Thuringia, where advanced manufacturing dominated pre-unification, the state is stepping forward to encourage private investment, developing an electric vehicle industry.[13]

Labour's promise to ramp up investment to £28 billion a year in climate investment is designed for this purpose, allowing every part of Britain to contribute to the national effort. Everybody benefits when the economy fires on all cylinders but the places that have been losers in the economic settlement are potentially those who gain the most. The road to net zero is paved with a million climate jobs – in wind, hydrogen, solar – meaning that the coastal and industrial towns where open space, waves, wind and engineering skills are in plentiful supply are particularly well placed to take advantage.

The state doesn't have to do all the heavy lifting but there is one area where it is irreplaceable: in tilting power towards those who are already rebuilding Britain from the ground up. Whether due to the unequal playing field for bricks-and-mortar businesses who are so often undercut by online retailers, or the companies – big and small – that pay badly, treat staff as expendable and extract wealth and investment from the local area, wealth creators are often undercut by wealth extractors. Governments stand idly by: afraid to grapple with the problem; feeling more pressure from the corporations themselves than from their own citizens; and fearful of the consequences faced by a country taking unilateral action to change the status quo. Most of us lose. The question is how to tilt the balance so that most of us gain.

This is not just a domestic issue. In a modern economy, where Marx and Engels' predictions about global corporations becoming more powerful than nation states is now a reality, how to reassert democracy is one of the great challenges of our age. During the last Labour leadership contest I floated the idea of a social licence for companies that would recognise the value they add, assess the social impact they have, and tilt the playing field towards those businesses who make a contribution to their country and communities. But every time a government shows leadership by insisting on rights for workers or proper payment of tax, it is threatened with the prospect of promised investment going elsewhere, of companies 'offshoring' their operations, or moving their headquarters. This is how, for four decades, corporate tax rates have been falling across the developed world. In Britain corporation tax fell dramatically from over 50 per cent in 1980 to less than 20 per cent in 2020. Companies can effectively shop around for lower tax rates and do business in one country but then shift their profits to another, more favourable, country. While a few people gain, money bleeds out of communities that are crying out for investment.

But in 2021, after four years of intense negotiations, US President Joe Biden made a breakthrough. A total of 136 countries, representing 90 per cent of global GDP, including Ireland, Estonia and Hungary, agreed to implement a global minimum corporation tax. From April 2023 multinationals will pay tax where they operate and earn profits and face a floor on competition over corporate income tax, ending an unchallenged four-decade-long race to the bottom, and returning $150 billion in lost revenues to exchequers across the world. The job is only half done. At the last moment, big concessions – an achingly long implementation time and a drastic cut in the rate of tax from 21 per cent to 15 per cent – were agreed. But national governments coming together to reassert the interest of people over profit was a rare and welcome sight in a globalised and digitalised twenty-first-century economy. The US treasury secretary, Janet Yellen, described it as a once-in-a-generation victory for economic diplomacy. It should not be the last. When national governments use global policy to invest in their own people, we move one step closer to the society described by R.H. Tawney 'in which a higher value will be set on human beings and a lower value on money and economic power when money and power do not serve economic ends'.

THE SOCIAL PARTNERSHIP

In 2020, history was made when the chancellor, the director general of the CBI and the general secretary of the TUC emerged from 10 Downing Street to announce the biggest economic stimulus in living memory. The Coronavirus Job Retention Scheme, or 'furlough' as it became known, has already cost the Treasury more than £69 billion and supported more than 11 million jobs. But just as striking as the size of the intervention was the sight of the leaders of the economy, business and the workforce standing together in the centre of power, a brief re-emergence of a lost tradition – tripartism – once dominant in British politics but unseen for almost four decades. It was treated as a one-off event, an exceptional measure – it took a global pandemic to persuade a Tory Government that we should work together in common cause.

We all have a stake in the country's success. But I believe we cannot succeed without the contribution of all of us. This principle – that building Britain was a partnership – was once much more central to the running of the economy.

In at least one part of the UK, it still is. In Wales, even before the pandemic raged, the Welsh Government had reached for tripartism to help rebuild the foundations of good work. The Social Partnership and Public Procurement Bill has brought Government, trade unions and employers together to address issues affecting the workforce – a success story held back only by the lack of powers the Welsh Government has been able to prise from Whitehall's grip. In Eastern Germany I was struck by how the federal system enabled far greater cooperation between workers, business owners and politicians because they were all united in the common goal of reviving their towns, cities, villages and regions. This was no attempt to recreate the communist era of command and control. In Bad Tabarz the mayor is reviving the local economy through the 'Bad Tabarz pound', which can be earned through volunteering and spent locally, and enlisted the entire town to protect and run the local assets which are the anchor of the local economy.

THE ASSET SOCIETY

The divide between those places and people who have assets and those who do not is now the biggest and most consequential divide in Britain.

It was apparent during the pandemic and the financial crash that assets help us to weather the storm, providing a safety net when times are bad and giving us the security to take risks and make choices when times are good.

The only thing stopping us from changing this is cowardice.

Take home ownership, currently at its lowest level in a generation, with too many people trapped in a private rented sector that increasingly resembles the wild west.

The system we have built allows cash rich investors to muscle out first-time buyers, pushing up prices way beyond the reach of local incomes. The cost of borrowing is 52 per cent higher for those without a deposit. Meanwhile the business model of many developers means they profit from rising prices and the market for land is built on an assumption of ever-increasing values. Developers face almost no pressure to compete on quality or innovation. The incentive (even for those who would wish it otherwise) is to slash costs so as to overpay for the most profitable plots of land. This leaves us with poor quality development in the wrong places, which in turn makes councils more resistant to development, squeezing the supply of land again and raising prices.

This is how we have failed to provide a generation with the foundations of a decent, secure life, treating housing as a speculative investment asset rather than as a place to live.

We have been failed by politicians who are so afraid of the taboo around the green belt that they have presided over the loss of large tracts of the nature-rich greenfield land which protects the character of local communities, while neglected scrubland and poor-quality ex-industrial land goes unused. Such was the case with a disused petrol station in Tottenham, where building was turned down because it is technically part of the green belt.

These politicians lack the will or imagination to take on a system rigged in favour of cash-rich speculators, and against first-time buyers, when state-backed mortgage insurance could allow access to homeownership for those who pay rent faithfully for years but are unable to save up for a deposit.

They refuse to challenge a land market that inflates prices, incentivises speculation over productive investment and allows money to bleed out of the system. Compulsory purchase rules must be reformed so that speculators can no longer command inflated prices for land way beyond market rates. Instead, we would usher in a new generation of local development corporations, spearheaded by and accountable to communities, replacing a reactive and overly adversarial approach to new housebuilding with a partnership in which communities, state and business work hand in hand to get the housing we need, built when we need it and where we need it.

I continue to be astonished by the reaction of some people in my own party who say home ownership is not a central concern of progressive politicians.

If you want people to have real resilience in their lives, they need their own assets – like a home or the child savings funds set up by the last Labour Government – and they need common assets, like council housing, which provides a secure home for life and can be handed down to future generations, or the credit unions and building societies that sustained and supported us over a century.

That is why the Right to Buy – whose abolition has come to be a totemic issue for many on the left – was originally a Labour policy aimed at extending assets and security to millions while not just replacing the council houses that were sold, but hugely expanding them.

The Thatcher Government's refusal to replace sold council housing stock disastrously pitted the rights of the individual against the rights of the community, costing us 1 million social homes in just a decade. On current rates of social rent delivery that would take around 150 years to replace.

There is no more perfect example of how a strategy to extend assets to the many has become a way of extracting and taking, rent-seeking, by a few for a few. In 2016 a Select Committee report found 40 per cent of homes sold under right to buy had found their way into the hands of private landlords who were extracting high rents at lower quality.

As Maurice Glasman says, capital is not democratic; it has a tendency to centralise.

That is why rebuilding and restoring what John Maynard Keynes called intermediary institutions, belonging neither to state nor market but to us all, matters hugely. They would democratise the economic realm.

They are our civic inheritance, will bolster us through the storms ahead. They will enable us to command the economic power in our communities that is essential to taking back control of our own lives, our communities and our country. This is what underpins a real commitment to community power and how to build a country that belongs to the creators, the makers, the doers and the builders.

THE LOCAL

In 2016, The Wellfield Hotel in Beech Hill, Wigan, was threatened with closure. It seemed almost inevitable that locals would suffer the same fate as other communities across the country who have lost their pubs over recent years. Even before the pandemic, eighteen pubs were closing a week. The Wellfield was the last local pub standing; the two other pubs on the estate had been lost to housing and a major supermarket chain. More than just bricks and mortar, The Wellfield was cherished – home to christening parties, wedding receptions and funeral wakes over the years. 'Everyone's got stories about the place,' the landlord told the local paper. 'My mum and dad had their wedding reception here and my dad came in every day until he died.' These are the institutions that the Conservative MP Jesse Norman wrote, 'help to shape and define us as we shape and define them'.[14] They have little value to those totting up numbers on a balance sheet in Whitehall but they anchor us and allow us to build those bonds that are the basis of a moral economy.

As developers circled, the pub's regulars went door to door with a petition trying to mobilise people power to defend what was rightfully theirs. But it was the local councillors who realised that – in this case – the law was on their side and launched a bid to have the pub designated as an 'asset of community value'. With the application successful, the change of use was denied and the pub would remain a pub. Later that year, under new ownership and restored to its former glory, The Wellfield was voted Wigan's Pub of the Year. For once, those who had a stake in it, who cared for it and understood its value, held the power to determine its future because national government had handed the community the tools to do it. This is the untapped force that enables a country to build the future from the foundations. We should spread this principle much more widely.

But progress is achingly slow. Take football, where it is widely recognised and understood that the fans should come first but too often come last. Measures to tilt power away from those who extract value and back towards those who build and sustain their clubs have failed. When clubs go into administration, fans must be given the chance to buy their own club. But what does this mean in reality to people who are asked to raise millions with just weeks to do it? The paucity of these measures is demonstrated by the stark fact that no team in the Premier League or Championship is wholly or partially fan owned. The fans do not hold money, so they cannot hold power. Owners are, as the Conservative MP Tracy Crouch, who recently completed a fan-led review of football, says, simply the 'custodians of a community asset'.[15] She proposed a licensing system to protect clubs and give greater representation to fans, including a 'golden share' to allow them to veto the sale of key club heritage items, the stadium and the name. So far, there is little sign the principles behind these recommendations have been widely understood by those who hold power, but she is right and we should restore this to the centre of our thinking, or we may wake up one day and find the things that make us who we are, are gone.

Despite this there is a quiet patriotism at work across Britain, people using the limited tools available to defend and build strong, thriving communities. They are at the forefront of the fight to ensure the assets that matter to us and belong to us are used for our collective benefit. It should not be a fight. When people have a stake, they build things that last. One of the lessons of thirteen years of Labour government is that the energy cooperative owned and run by hundreds of local people survives a change of government while the Sure Start services designed and funded from Whitehall do not.

Yet the buses, hospitals, social care and postal services, trains, water and energy that were once owned by us in common have been outsourced or sold off piece by piece over the last four decades. I have long believed our railways are best run by the state. It is surely absurd that any other government around the world can run our railways except our own. And I share Michael Sandel's view that allowing market economics to permeate education, healthcare and other social goods has cost us dearly. But in the furious debate that has followed – whether the market or the state should provide – we seem to have forgotten about people.

In 2016, serving as Labour's shadow energy secretary I asked at the Labour Party Conference to put people back in charge of one of our public assets – energy. This was six years before Russia invaded Ukraine and the full scale of the UK's broken approach to energy became apparent, but the warning signs were already there for anyone who cared to see them. I told the conference we needed a radical new approach to democratise the energy market: 'There should be nothing to stop every community in this country owning its own clean energy power station. Across the country, schools are already taking the initiative and going solar – generating power and heat for their own use. With the right support, community-based energy companies and cooperatives could be a new powerhouse, and a path to a more secure energy future – to work with our local government leaders to push for a clean energy boom in our great cities. Because our city and county regions can lead the world. They can point the way towards a safer, brighter, more secure future. To be the light on the hill for all of us who care about the cost of our energy – to our family budgets, our businesses and our environment. Let's not wait for this government. Because let's face it, we'd be waiting forever. Let's seize the initiative and put power into our own hands. The transformation of the way our world powers its economy – how we turn on every light, how we drive every car, how we heat our homes and keep our phones and computers running – is already one of the great stories of human endeavour. I want it to be a story people across Britain can be proud of. I want the names of British inventors and companies stamped on wind-turbines, solar panels and electric cars. I want our people to own a stake in this future, and to feel proud of the contribution they have made towards the safety and wellbeing of our children, and the health of our planet.'

I made that speech at a moment when the government had recently pulled funding for ground-breaking carbon capture and storage schemes in Aberdeenshire and Yorkshire and would shortly cancel the Swansea Bay Tidal Lagoon, a project which would have powered 150,000 Welsh homes for 120 years and create thousands of jobs.[16] These are the sorts of schemes that allow communities to build resilience in their economy, create and protect good jobs and cut carbon emissions, but can be cancelled at one stroke of a pen by ministers sitting in Whitehall.

This is what has convinced me that the only answer is far greater financial autonomy for all parts of Britain. The promise to 'level up' has become a Hunger Games-style contest forcing local leaders to slug it out for small grants dictated from Whitehall and communities who live or die at the whim of a Tory chancellor who promises to level up one day and govern like Thatcher the next.

Taking ownership of assets protects the social fabric and generates revenue to allow places to stand on their own two feet. But too often rights on paper don't translate into action. The problem is money. When Wigan Athletic went into administration we had the right to buy it, but only if we could find £16 million. This is why only fifteen of every 1000 assets designated assets of community value eventually make it into community ownership.[17]

We should replace the right to bid for assets – like football clubs, live music venues and pubs – with a far more powerful community right to buy, giving places first refusal on assets of community value and long-term vacant high street property and the right to buy them without competition – with longer to raise the money too. If land or buildings are in a state of significant disrepair, we should have the right to force their sale – we should not have to stand by and watch as our communities fall apart.

At the moment there is a small Community Ownership Fund which is held by Whitehall. We should ensure that every community has not just a fund to draw on but the ability to generate revenue for the community too. In Plymouth the Council's support was vital in getting Plymouth Community Energy up and running. Anyone over eighteen can buy community shares. The revenue goes back into the community. In Scotland, Huntly Development Trust have used measures pioneered by the last Labour Government to bring land back into community hands to be used for the good of all the people, not just some. Their community-owned wind farm generates revenue which is then reinvested in the town. From Birmingham to Grimsby communities are investing in housing, using the proceeds to rebuild their communities and invest in the people within them.

This is the first step on the way to greater financial auton-omy for our towns, villages and cities. Whether land, housing or energy, high street shops, football clubs or live music venues, these assets raise revenue to be used and passed down through the generations, driven by the wishes of the commu-nity, held in common and used for the common good.

I've seen it in action in Hendon in the North East of England. Recent decades have not been kind to this proud community. Rogue landlords were allowed to buy up the cottages which are typical in this part of Sunderland, letting them out to people who could not cope alone. As they struggled to survive, buildings fell into disrepair and the neighbourhood struggled to absorb the social fallout.

Brutal cuts to council budgets left many buildings empty, like the much-loved historic library which stands in the centre of the village. But thanks to local people, it is back in use. It was there that I met a community group whose treatment of its tenants is changing lives. They have bought up properties as they become vacant, restored them and let them out to the people who need them. When I visited on a Friday morning it was bustling. I listened as one of the tenants told me how she approached Back on the Map after her relationship broke down, at her lowest ebb. She had children, no deposit and every door had been slammed in her face. She wept as she talked about the sheer hopelessness of it all. She told me, 'If this had been an agency, I would be homeless right now.' The money generated by these activities has allowed them to invest in new housing and in local people, in a place that was once the economic heart of a city built on glass, coal and shipbuilding. They call themselves Back on the Map in recognition of what they have contributed, how much they still do and how much more they are determined to achieve.

THE FINANCIAL INSTITUTIONS WE NEED

Those brilliant women at Back on the Map would have once known exactly who would help them meet their ambitions. Northern Rock was a building society built by the people of the North East to serve the people of the North East. Slowly and steadily it came to play a central role in a region that was, with its mines and shipyards, central to the future of the UK. It was that most precious of institutions, part of our civic inheritance, a trusted financial institution that supported its region's families to own their own homes and help their businesses to grow. Through its community foundation it was a key plank in the rich civic life to which the people of the North East laid claim. In 1997 it demutualised and floated on the London Stock Exchange. Its business model left it highly exposed in the wake of the financial crash, and by 2007 it had collapsed. Nationalised by a Labour Government and sold off by the Coalition Government that followed, its loss was a direct consequence of the decision to demutualise and a series of choices that put short-term gain for a few before the long-term, collective benefits of a historic shared institution.

This was an institution that had partnered its region through tough times and good for 150 years, weathering four major recessions and emerging stronger from each. It provided hope to striking miners and their families when it suspended mortgage payments in the 1980s. When it collapsed, its sponsorship deal with Newcastle United was taken up by Wonga, a company that at its height was lending at rates of 5,852 per cent to those who could not find cheaper credit elsewhere.[18]

But the lesson of Northern Rock and its long success is that institutions which are rooted in their communities, where people have a stake in their success and they have a stake in the community's, can do incredible things. Over a decade after it was allowed to collapse, there are calls to recreate its role through a British Investment Bank, regional investment banks or decentralised citizen's wealth funds[19] to spread power, prosperity and opportunity much more widely.

This has become pressing. The last decade has seen an acceleration of the departure of banks from what were successful local economies, sometimes for short-term cost cutting, but underpinned by a lazy assumption that some parts of the country are just more productive than others. This is not an assumption limited to banks. In 2007 a think tank report named Cities Unlimited said 'the only way towns and cities that are less well connected ... can compete to attract firms is to accept lower wages'.[20] They 'need to accept above all that we cannot guarantee to regenerate every town and every city in Britain that has fallen behind ... We cannot, with the best will in the world, move JP Morgan to Blackburn, or Deutsche Bank to Sunderland ... We may wish it otherwise, but we know that it will not happen. London is London ... We believe therefore that part of the solution to urban regeneration in areas far from London is to allow London to grow, so that some of the people living in those areas are able to migrate to London.' The author went on to work for then chancellor of the exchequer Rishi Sunak.[21]

Recent research by the University of Sheffield has debunked the idea that London and the South East outstrips the rest of the country in terms of economic efficiency. There is virtually no difference in economic efficiency between workers in different regions or between workers in cities and towns. In fact, the dominance of some regions can have a dampening effect: the same research suggests that the City has sucked growth out of the regional economy to the tune of £4,500 billion over the last twenty years. If the financial sector was smaller, and if finance were more focused on supporting other areas of the economy, the UK may have seen greater growth overall.[22]

Instead of spreading and creating wealth through investment, too much of our banking system extracts it from places and people. In 2017 loans to UK businesses accounted for just 5 per cent of UK bank assets compared to 78 per cent for property loans.[23] A centralised remote banking system, left in the hands of those who have no stake in the future of communities across Britain, has left us with an overexposed national economy highly dependent on the property bubble, and this has not changed, despite a financial crash in 2008 which cost people's homes, pensions and life savings. When the whole thing came crashing down, guess who lost?

A study of 14,000 banks in the US found that large banks tend to lend to large firms while small banks tended to lend to small firms. There are 1.875 million businesses in London and the South East; 154,000 in the North East. Small banks, back in communities, would support small businesses and spread power and opportunity more widely. But we are heading in the wrong direction.

Almost half of all bank branches across the country have closed since 2015.[24] Banks argue that they are responding to customers moving online but that still leaves millions of people in rural areas, and small and medium-sized towns, without the banking services they need. Often people are directed to use a Post Office that is also under threat of closure. This was precisely my experience in Wigan. That Post Office was closed. It relocated to WH Smith, which itself closed a few years later.

Hundreds of communities across Britain are now effectively banking in ATM 'deserts' as thousands of branches and ATMs close every year.[25] On 7 April 2000, ninety villages in the country lost their only bank in a single day of closures from Barclays Bank.

Banks are vital community assets and deserve to be treated as such in law. The small local bank, which understands the circumstances and cares of the local economy, has a value that deserves to be protected. There are community banks and credit unions across the country, owned by and answerable to the public and not shareholders or financial investors. The Welsh Government has moved forward with plans to support Banc Cambria, a community bank aiming to operate across Wales and fill the space left by bank branch closures.[26]

Across America, dozens of community banks either already exist or are preparing for roll-out and in Europe, too, the public-owned bank is a routine part of daily life in Germany, France and Italy. Alongside Banc Cambria, there are tentative plans to open such publicly owned and publicly run community banks in Greater Manchester, the North West, South West and Northern Ireland.[27] But too often they compete on an uneven playing field with the bigger banks.

In the United States a national government stepped up to level the playing field as far back as the 1970s. It was in response to a trend of banks departing many areas of the country, cutting off poorer and more remote communities, many of them predominantly African Americans.

Campaigners used the law to set this right. The Community Reinvestment Act was introduced to ensure banks served the credit needs of low-income communities, including the need to have a geographical presence. Some twenty-five years on, proposals are on the table which seek to update it for the modern age. This is government doing its job as the custodian of public interest to support those who invest over those who extract wealth from the places we call home.

Places matter. They ground and anchor us and give life colour and meaning. But just as some people have been cut out of their fair share, so have places. Those places have been invisible to national decision makers for too long.

In 2017 the Industrial Strategy Commission reported: 'The UK is by far the most regionally unequal EU economy. All core cities outside London, with the exception of Bristol and Aberdeen, have productivity lower than the national average. Many de-industrialised areas, often on the fringes of city regions, present apparently intractable combinations of social, educational and economic problems while some of the most deprived communities are to be found on the coasts and in rural peripheries. Most economies have a small number of very large, dense and highly productive city regions. The UK is unique amongst OECD member states in only having one, London. Not having a second or third large urban region leads to high congestion costs in the capital, draws highly productive activity and jobs from elsewhere in the UK to London, and requires policy actions to be taken to prevent overheating earlier than would be desirable for other regions.'[28]

The Treasury has recently written place-based assessment into the Green Book – guidance issued on how to appraise policies, programmes and projects. It was a good idea that so far has had little practical effect. What's required is a complete change in mindset, a change to what we value and how we measure success.

EVERYTHING EXCEPT THAT WHICH MAKES LIFE WORTHWHILE

In her short but brilliant book, *GDP: A Brief but Affectionate History*, the economist Diane Coyle argues that the increasing use of GDP as a shorthand for how well we're doing is a problem. It doesn't work, not least because a World War II economy was able to measure the goods that came off the assembly line far more easily than a digitised globalised economy. What's more, it renders so many of the things that matter completely invisible. Currently GDP tells us nothing about the 'everyday economy' – the goods and services like childcare and health services that make up a significant proportion of our activity (some estimates put the figure as high as 40 per cent). Yet, strikingly, many European countries saw their GDP increase when prostitution and drugs were included in measurements of market activity. Inequality has grown sharply since the 1980s, and climate change poses the greatest threat to our collective future but GDP tells us nothing about the distribution of growth or the sustainability of the economy.

Bobby Kennedy was among the first to recognise this problem. 'The Gross National Product does not allow for the health of our children, the quality of their education or the joy of their play. It does not include the beauty of our poetry or the strength of our marriages, the intelligence of our public debate or the integrity of our public officials. It measures neither our wit nor our courage, neither our wisdom nor our learning, neither our compassion nor our devotion to our country, it measures everything, in short, except that which makes life worthwhile.'[29]

'We are in a statistical fog,' Coyle writes. GDP matters: 'For all its flaws, it is still a bright light shining through the mist,' but she is right to say that using it as a hallmark, not just of economic success but social success too, is not the way to get Britain working again.

By adjusting the lens, we can bring the things that matter back into focus. In 2007 UNICEF published a groundbreaking study looking at the wellbeing of children and young people in some of the world's richest countries.[30] Researchers asked questions that compared life for children in twenty-one different countries – from Poland to the United States. They looked at things like child poverty, health, education, where children lived and their safety. They also looked at risk factors like violence, smoking, alcohol and drugs that can affect how children live their lives. But most importantly, they asked children how they felt about their own lives.

The New Labour years were a golden era in the prioritisation of children. Record investment in education and investment in early years programmes like Sure Start, Every Child Matters and Aim Higher had opened up opportunities and lifted a million children out of poverty. For the first time, many young people had the chance to go to university, and record numbers took it. Teenage pregnancy rates were down, drug use was down and children in care became a priority for the first time. But when UNICEF published their report, shockingly it turned out that children and young people in Britain were among the unhappiest in the developed world in the early years of the new millennium.

The findings were a wake-up call for government and for all those responsible for the wellbeing of our children and young people. When the report landed, I was working at The Children's Society and the response from Government was fascinating. Instead of seeking to rubbish the report, or reel off the statistics about many Government successes, they enlisted our help and many others, putting our heads together to try and figure out what was wrong. The answer led us to commit to the biggest ongoing conversation with children in our 125-year history. They told us that friends and family were the things that mattered most, but too often the system drove a coach and horses through those things at the moment they most mattered. Children in care were taken from their families for their own safety but then moved miles away to a foster care placement, in the process losing contact with the one person – a teacher, a friend, a much-loved grandparent – who might have sustained them. This is how the Wellbeing Index was born. It was used by the Labour Government to supplement measures like GDP and continued to be used by the Cameron Government that followed. Cameron was criticised by 'traditionalists' for continuing to use it but surely wellbeing can tell us more about the health of our nation than the amount of market activity in prostitution. While GDP puts an economic value on cutting down a forest, other measures like wellbeing help us measure the value of protecting it.

One way we might refocus the lens is by taking a different, place-based approach to the economy.

For decades there has been an assumption in both the US and the UK that interventions should be what is known as 'space-blind' rather than 'place-based'. The theory was that people naturally move to more prosperous places – known in the US as 'the big sort' – to find opportunity. Moreover, the Reagan administration argued that a place-based approach was regressive, helping wealthier people in poorer areas. By focusing solely on individuals, America would be better off. The political upheavals in the US, UK, France, Germany and elsewhere have flipped this on its head. Now there is a recognition, even amongst its biggest champions,[31] that the space-blind approach has written off too many places, underplayed the positive role social capital, place and community can play in economic growth, and created a self-reinforcing spiral of decline as some places fall further and further behind, in turn becoming less able to weather capital shocks like the 2008 financial crash or COVID.[32]

It is this change of approach that has produced a fascinating idea – Universal Basic Infrastructure, championed by the Industrial Strategy Commission, Diane Coyle and the academic, Andy Westwood.[33] They propose a per capita formula, below which services may not fall – GP surgeries, police stations, childcare, schools, Post Offices, banks, broadband and libraries. Once they reach a minimum per population size, local services may not close or reduce below minimum standards in national or regional decision making. This could be delivered by writing minimum universal standards into companies' licence to operate or contract. The focus on places is deliberate.

They write: 'Universal Credit (or even a Universal Basic Income) will not help people access a decent education system or a functional bus network. Effective policy for levelling up involves a much deeper understanding of the links between public and private sectors, civic institutions and the value of the networks in communities. It demands a shift in the way we think about infrastructure, institutions and people and about the government's role in supporting them.'[34]

Their suggestion is designed, at one stroke, to protect things that have been neglected: the one village shop or pub, without which we are cut off from the essentials of a good life; childcare, which is not currently recognised as an essential plank of the country's infrastructure; and the buses and trains that connect us to apprenticeships and grandchildren, choices and chances.

Those buses and trains have become a hot political issue in recent years, crumbling or non-existent across large swathes of the country. A 2019 report found that the gap between London and the North grew over the last decade, with spending growing by 2.5 times more per person in London and leaving the North short-changed by £66 billion. How could it be then that instead of setting this right the Government planned to hand seven times more to people in London than those in the North East of England in the future?[35]

In the search to increase productivity, bodies like the National Infrastructure Commission put their limited resources where there is something to build on – the transport, digital and skills infrastructure which has come from years of investment. This is how they get more bang for their buck in pursuit of the productivity 'miracle' but it is also how some places pull further ahead while others continue to fall further behind.

This mindset is now so widespread that even where productivity would be far better served by investment elsewhere, it is assumed it wouldn't. A 2018 study called 'The Imperial Treasury' revealed that even better investments outside of London and the South East don't get a look in. The headlong rush towards productivity gains also risks erasing people in large parts of our economy. Governments rightly focus on jobs in the new economy in fields like analytics, IT, robotics and green energy but most people work in the everyday economy in jobs like retail, healthcare, public services, education, tourism and hospitality. These are jobs which matter but are not well served by measures of productivity. They are either difficult to quantify or written off as unproductive altogether.

This is particularly acute in areas where it is harder to improve productivity, like social care. Attempts to do so can have appalling consequences, like the recent practice of scheduling fifteen-minute appointments, with few breaks in between. Social care workers perform the most crucial of roles in an ageing population but they are amongst the worst-paid and poorly protected in our economy, frequently classified as 'unproductive'. An approach that reduces us all to mere 'producers' is misguided and outmoded. The contribution we make should matter more than the amount of output we can measure. We should rethink what we are trying to achieve. Imagine how different it would be if our goal shifted to providing the best quality care in the world?

Wales's Labour Government has taken the lead in this area. Combining a focus on the foundational economy – recognizing the value of social care to the overall economy and pledging to protect it – with a strategy to upskill and modernize the way social workers operate that across Wales has had some success in reaching people who need help and reducing avoidable pressures on social carers. But for the most part governments have proven unresponsive, even in the face of rising discontent, anger and political upheaval. Big corporations have fought tooth and nail to hang on to economic power and people who have tried to build a different settlement from the ground up have been thwarted by a system that is rigged against them. This is what accounts for the alienation many people still feel. Fifty years ago at Glasgow University the trade unionist Jimmy Reid addressed this theme in a speech which was to echo through the decades that followed.[36]

'The untapped resources of the North Sea are as nothing to the untapped resources of our people. I am convinced that the great mass of our people go through life without even a glimmer of what they could have contributed to their fellow human beings. This is a personal tragedy. It is a social crime. The flowering of each individual's personality and talents is the precondition for everyone's development.'

'Reject the rat race,' he urged the students. 'A rat race is for rats.'

6.

OF THE PEOPLE, FOR THE PEOPLE, BY THE PEOPLE, WITH THE PEOPLE

'A state which dwarfs its men, in order that they may be more docile instruments in its hands even for beneficial purposes – will find that with small men no great thing can really be accomplished.'

John Stuart Mill

Politics isn't working. Whether it's the football fans who stand to lose their club, the hospital workers who stand to lose their vocation or the young people who stand to lose their freedom, those who have the most at stake too often have the least say. Millions of micro-decisions that directly and deeply affect our lives, our families, our communities and our country are made by a small number of people and institutions that are too often unresponsive, unaccountable – even unidentifiable.

When this many people feel deep in their bones that democracy isn't working, we have to take it seriously. The warning lights have been flashing for over a decade but we have refused to heed them, even as we have experienced waves of populism, separatism and political earthquakes on both sides of the Atlantic – a roar of noise that politicians couldn't hear because they had become so deeply disconnected from the people they represent.

My view is simple: hand decisions to people who have a stake in the outcome, and things get better. I often think of the many parents of disabled children who have been through my constituency surgery over the last decade. Without a single exception, regardless of their own background, every single one had become an expert in opaque systems and medical advances that only a few years previously would have seemed impossible. With so much at stake, they fought harder, worked longer and are to this day amongst the most creative people I've met, relentlessly solving problems.

One of those mums, Alex Johnson, whose child Jack has been diagnosed with the degenerative condition Duchenne Muscular Dystrophy, has raised millions for medical research and enlisted the whole of Wigan in the fight. She became such an expert in the condition that she was asked to join the board that guided decisions about clinical trials across the European Union. Never daunted, when a handful of corporations dominated the wheelchair market, keeping costs sky high and disincentivising advances, she and co-founder Emily Crossley enlisted the charity WhizzKids to design and launch their own.

She and others like her have taught me that, in every walk of life, people will go to extraordinary lengths to build and defend the businesses, town centres, healthcare and educational opportunities that make a world of difference to them and their families. Theirs is the great untapped power in our country. The refusal to break open decision making and put power back in their hands holds our whole country back. If we were designing a political system from scratch, we sure as hell wouldn't start from here.

We can't just keep tinkering. We need to fundamentally reimagine our political system to build on the quiet patriotism at work in every community that inspires people to create, defend and build things that matter, sometimes with the backing of their national, local or regional government, but too often despite it. They are driven by a pride and belief in what they, their families, their community and their country can be. They are the ambitious ones. They need political leaders as ambitious as they are.

I have grown tired of a political debate in which leading politicians say Westminster is fundamentally fine, or that Westminster is broken. Their analysis is too thin, their answers too shallow. On one side of this debate there is a refusal to acknowledge that, starved of legitimacy, representative democracy is dying; on the other, an argument that this malaise only affects national government, when so many of the problems afflict local, regional and federal government too.

Government matters. It must guard, defend and promote the public realm so that we never allow 'might to become right'. Its central job, to ensure nobody can hoard money and power and minority rights are defended, is one that matters but is seldom done. Whether it's the Biden administration's collective agreement on a global minimum corporation tax, or Wigan Council's The Deal, the best kind of government takes its instruction from the people, and coordinates action to those ends.

Abraham Lincoln famously proclaimed government 'of the people, by the people, for the people.' I believe we need government with the people. A partnership puts people, their objectives and concerns in the driving seat and ensures that decisions which affect us are taken in the interests of the common good.

We haven't seen much of this in recent years. If anything, politics from left to right, Liberal to Conservative, has headed in the wrong direction, while people are heading in the other, embracing a different kind of politics and the politicians that embody it. So much of this stems from a political culture that tries to exert a tight managerial grip. It won't work. Politics is complicated because we are complicated. Decision making will be messy because life is messy. We need a culture that can accept complexity and embrace difference, manage conflict – far more open, responsible and accountable and with leadership to match. When was the last time you heard a politician say they got it wrong, they've changed their mind, they just don't know? When they do, they're slammed for U-turning. As I saw at the Paris Climate Conference, good leaders have the self-confidence to listen and to change.

We need new institutions fit for this stormy age. They must be partners to the people: open, willing and able to be challenged. In short, we need to fundamentally reimagine the role of the state. The Cameron years, and its harsh, deep cuts to public spending, sparked a heated debate about the size of the state but we never paused to ask, instead of big or small, what about different? The devolution reforms made under four successive prime ministers should have asked where fundamentally power should lie but it has collapsed into a debate about which group of men – in Whitehall or the town hall – should make decisions on our behalf. I say this isn't good enough. Power lies with people and must be returned.

In discussions about this I have often been reminded that our political system has never lived up to this ideal. My response is, why not? In every part of Britain there are people pointing the way. They show how communities who are in the driving seat of their own places and lives regain control, and with that comes an ease and self-confidence that allows them to strike out and do things differently, spurring them on to greater things. This is the basis of a successful country, one that trusts in the wisdom and knowledge of its people. This is the new politics. This is the future of Britain.

WHAT ABOUT THE PEOPLE?

In November 2014 the chancellor George Osborne announced a radical new devolution deal for Greater Manchester, a political construct made up of the cities of Manchester and Salford, plus eight Lancashire and Cheshire towns whose leaders had long worked together to solve shared challenges. Attempts by the previous Labour Government to establish elected assemblies had failed and Conservative proposals for city mayors in referendums across Britain, including in Manchester, had been roundly defeated. So this was hailed as a 'revolutionary moment', handing new powers and control of the budgets to a group of local government leaders in one of the most heavily centralised countries in the world.

But the photograph of the chancellor, the Police and Crime Commissioner and ten council leaders signing the deal into history also told another story. It showed twelve white men, smiling into the camera, in one of the most diverse parts of the country. Theirs was a deal negotiated behind closed doors, announced to the media and coming as a particular surprise to those residents who lived in the city of Manchester, who had rejected plans for a mayor just two years earlier. As mentioned above, the 'public consultation' only ran for three weeks, wasn't advertised and had just twelve responses, ten of which came from the same council leaders who had brokered the deal in the first place. The biggest plank of the deal – handing control over the NHS to local leaders – wasn't even mentioned.

Andy Burnham, the then shadow health secretary who would later go on to invigorate the devolution agenda as the popular mayor of Greater Manchester, opposed the deal and the way it was reached, calling it a 'Swiss cheese', full of holes.[1]

At the time I wrote, 'A binary choice between an unaccountable structure in London or another in Manchester is no choice at all.'[2] Many of the Labour leaders who signed the deal shared these concerns but the Government was clear: it was the only one on the table. So in a discussion about democracy, democracy had become an afterthought and a backroom deal about how we govern ourselves took out of the equation the best asset we have: the people.

When the BBC visited Wigan to ask people what they thought of 'Devo Manc', those they stopped to ask were completely baffled. They didn't even understand the question.

Devolution can and should bring significant benefits to places like Wigan because decisions made closer to people are usually better decisions. The assets and potential in places are almost always better understood by those closest to them.

This is how many of the new generation of regional leaders have approached the job. On a recent visit to Prescot in Merseyside, I was shown around by the metro mayor, Steve Rotherham. He had stepped forward to provide funding to help build Shakespeare North when the government's many 'levelling up' funds fell through. He told me, 'We were told people in Knowsley wouldn't come. But we knew they would.' He wasn't at all surprised when they were packed out during the opening weekend. He knew the community would embrace it because he had grown up just a few miles down the road. He didn't need to defeat any stereotypes because he never held any. He just got behind the people of Knowsley and their local leaders and together they showed who was right.

It was a reminder that where Whitehall often sees problems, we see potential. I heard an example of this as I met with local leaders in Birmingham as they prepared to host the 2022 Commonwealth Games. The games are run by a private limited company appointed by the government, with the leader of the Council the sole elected representative on it. The elected politicians told me of their horror when it was proposed that the medals for the games should be commissioned overseas. Birmingham has been home to the Jewellery Quarter for 350 years – a buzzing, vibrant place, which produces over half of all the UK's handmade jewellery. This is a legacy and contribution that deserves recognition and respect. In the end, the medals were produced by students at the Jewellery Quarter and offer a visible, beautiful symbol of what Birmingham has to offer. It is a reminder of how much it matters that decisions are made by those who understand not just the challenges, but the strengths, assets and skills in every place.

Real devolution is a chance to move away from remote, technocratic government that allows people to make decisions from afar, clueless about the impact on others they will never know in places they have never been.

Devolution in Britain is a job not yet done. It still leaves too many of us going cap in hand to Whitehall to beg for permission or resources to do things we know will work for us. Try boosting opportunities, good jobs and wages without control over what you can spend – or public transport, skills policy and the rollout of broadband. The Government has said it will fix this, but the much-vaunted Levelling Up White Paper that Michael Gove and the Conservative Government unveiled in February 2022 did nothing of the sort. Power and money remain in the iron grip of a small group of ministers and civil servants in Whitehall and the agenda has been quietly junked in government.[3] In fact, for all the talk, the story of the last decade has been one of centralisation. It has been missed in a debate dominated by resources, but when the government abolished its long-promised plan to extend new rail services across the North of England, it wasn't just the funding that was pulled back to Whitehall but also the powers to deliver what was left of it.

We should end the situation where areas compete for the right to repatriate limited powers from Whitehall and legislate to flip the presumption of power closer to the people, into the hands of those who know how to use it. We should put local communities in charge of their own destiny, and provide that opportunity to all places, not just some.

Housing, energy and the environment are central to local growth and the transition to net zero. Cornwall's devolution deal has shown how moving power can support the creation of hundreds of energy-efficient homes. There, regional and local leaders control (or exert great influence) over a third of carbon emissions,[4] which is why the mayor of the West Midlands Andy Street is pushing for them to take control of funding and set carbon budgets for which they could be held to account.[5]

Birmingham, London and Manchester have been pushing for the right to levy a hotel bed tax, which many major global cities use to raise money and reinvest in the local area, but requests for the power to levy this charge on visitors have been repeatedly ignored by Whitehall.

People in Cumbria are crying out for transport improvements to connect with friends, family, jobs and healthcare. The county's roads, rail and buses are all under so much strain that a few years ago at the height of the Northern Rail chaos, when Northern Trains cancelled the entire rail service, the local MP, Tim Farron, resorted to bringing a heritage railway line back into use to ferry people to work. This year Cumbria was denied a single penny for its buses from the £1 billion government fund. When bus routes were later cancelled, the council said it was 'disappointed' but had no power or resources to do anything about it.

This highlights one of the biggest problems with devolution to date. Currently only 41 per cent of people in England are covered by a Mayoral Devolved Authority (only 14 per cent of England's land area).[6] For all the talk of local empowerment it has been the chancellor who decides from Whitehall which places will be invited to bid for new devolution deals, based on whether he believes they are 'functional economic areas'. If they are successful they are permitted a few new powers – but only if they accept a mayor. Leaving aside how offensive it is to be deemed not 'functional' by a chancellor who on a trip to Bury market thought he was in Burnley,[7] there are bigger principles at stake. People must consent to their own governance in a democracy or it is surely not a democracy at all. There is, after all, a long history of people in Britain rejecting top-down structures dreamt up in Westminster.[8]

There are many voices across the political spectrum calling for a menu of powers to be on offer to all, not just some, based on political arrangements imposed not from Whitehall but determined by people and reflective of economic geography and local identity.[9] They are right, but so far their calls have not been heeded. In South Yorkshire there was strong support for a devolution deal that reflected Yorkshire's identity. Both a South Yorkshire-wide Citizen's Assembly and community polls in Barnsley and Doncaster showed overwhelming support for a One Yorkshire deal over the Sheffield City Region model being proposed by the Government.[10] The popular regional mayor, Dan Jarvis, agreed and put One Yorkshire forward, only to see it rejected out of hand by a junior minister.

Many countries across the world have what is known as asymmetric devolution – different arrangements that respect the uniqueness and difference of places. Spain, for example, has written into its constitution that any region can establish an 'autonomous community', while Germany has a federal system with varying arrangements at local level. The UK already has asymmetric devolution, with different governance arrangements in Wales and Scotland, and different types of councils within England. The desire to force every place to follow the same route is arguably not a very British tradition. Critics say it leads to a postcode lottery but this is not inevitable. Whether it's Universal Basic Infrastructure, the 'kitemark' of minimum standards proposed by UNISON,[11] or universally established principles – that the NHS must remain free at the point of use, as the late (Lord) Bob Kerslake proposed – there are a host of ways to ensure nobody is left out or left behind in the future.[12] The only thing that is certain is that, right now, far too many of us are.

The best way to ensure we get the decisions we need is to empower us to choose, and hold accountable, leaders to deliver on that promise. Devolution should make this easier, but simply moving power from one group of men in Whitehall to another in the town hall doesn't, in and of itself, make it any easier to hold them to account for decisions. Ask many elected councillors in devolved areas, and they will tell you that despite their best efforts they aren't even afforded the respect of being told what decisions are being made.

A few years after that historic photograph in Manchester Town Hall, an independent review concluded devolution had brought tangible benefits to much of the sub-region. Leaders were able to better flex different funding streams to deliver their vision, planning was more coherent and the mayor had used his soft powers to great effect to convene, cajole and provide a national platform for Greater Manchester. But this has not been felt everywhere. In one particularly bleak report the *Manchester Evening News* talked to people involved in the project and concluded: 'Increasingly they believe the current system isn't fit for purpose, warning scrutiny meetings at Greater Manchester level are "tick box" exercises, gatherings that are frequently cancelled at the last minute and only hear from the mayor roughly once a year. One such committee, the "corporate issues and reform" panel, is supposed to scrutinise major public sector programmes across the city region. But it has not met formally since February, with meetings in March, July, September and on Tuesday this week all cancelled or held informally due to a lack of attendance.'[13] A Labour councillor who spoke anonymously said 'people didn't see it as adding value, because it didn't'.

This is a problem driven by structures, not people. The mayor of Greater Manchester, Andy Burnham, has reached out to people to bring them into the conversation, holding town hall meetings, appearing on radio phone-ins and using social media to communicate with the people he represents. It's been so successful that the government wants every mayor to follow suit. But this is their choice, when it should be our right. These are decisions about who gets the trains, buses and trams that connect us to jobs, education, friends and family. They determine who has to travel miles for mental health service provision and who gets it on their doorstep. And often we don't even know who is making these decisions. In 2021, a full seven years after the devolution deals began to be rolled out, a House of Commons Select Committee report warned that transparency and public engagement in devolution deals 'remain minimal'.[14] Surely we can do better than this?

If power and money is going to move to local places to enable us to do things for ourselves, then we need to put the people back into the picture, strengthening local accountability and providing communities and councillors with the tools and resources they need to scrutinise and challenge those who hold power. There is an urgency to this at local level where often there is only one political party making decisions and holding itself to account. It is curious to me why there has been an important debate about introducing proportional representation at Westminster but it is seldom up for discussion at local and regional level where the problem it seeks to solve is often more acute.

Devolution deals that replicate the centralising tendency are devolution in name only, those that, instead of pushing power out to people, pull power up. In the best cases, decisions have been made at scale when necessary and locally when possible. But in others, decisions that were made by individual councils have moved to a town hall dozens of miles away, as divorced from local context as the system they replaced. Efforts to centralise healthcare are a pressing example, moving decision making and services to major cities when the older people in need of those services live in the surrounding towns and the transport isn't there.

This is why local councillors need proper resources to hold their mayors and leaders to account, without fearing they will be removed from office. The prime minister doesn't appoint chairs of Select Committees so why is it that many council leaders appoint the chairs of those who scrutinise them?[15] Proposals to hand more money to local leaders to spend have been greeted with enthusiasm from politicians on left and right, but it is surely right that with greater responsibility comes more scrutiny, with resources dedicated to this as they are in Parliament. Nowhere at present is there is an equivalent of the Public Accounts Committee, whose formidable former chair Margaret Hodge used this powerful committee, armed with expertise and resources, to expose the waste, cronyism and dirty foreign money that is poisoning our democracy.

GO DEEPER

In 1994 the residents of Perry Common in Birmingham made a decision that was to save, then transform, the community they call home. The estate had been built in the 1920s but was by then structurally unsound. With their homes facing demolition, the residents' association fought back. I went to see them on a snowy winter's day as we campaigned to elect a successor to Jack Dromey, their former local MP and one of their great champions. The people I met there are amongst the most fun, energetic and infectiously optimistic I have ever come across. In contrast to the photograph of the Devo Manc deal, they looked and sounded like the people of Birmingham – of and for their community.

As we shivered in the entranceway to the beautifully restored Witton Lodge, they explained how a far-sighted council that had backed them early had been a game-changer. Birmingham Council gifted them the land on which their homes stood. The money from homes built by private developers allowed them to rebuild their own homes, and construct and manage a further 187 properties that they now rent out and run. The revenues fund a community hall – home to clubs and events, jobs and skills training – and an eco-hub, complete with an allotment that supplies fresh food to the local foodbank. The residents' association chair, Linda, told me: 'It belongs to the whole community, not just us. That's why it works.' But experiences like this are just far too rare, even locally, where too many people feel their leaders still try to hang on to power.

For more people to do what the residents of Perry Common have done, they need resources and power but they also need knowledge. I've lost count of the number of times I've been into secondary schools over the years and heard young people say they wouldn't have the first idea where to start in making change in their own lives, community or country. But I've seen too how it can be done, as in a local primary school where I saw the UNICEF Rights Respecting School programme in practice. I will admit to having been sceptical as five-year-olds gathered to debate how to spend the school budget for new play equipment. But the headteacher was clear, the decision was theirs – and the ideas were pretty spectacular. At first they voted for a rollercoaster, until they realised that would blow the entire school budget and take up more space than the playground and school grounds combined. After much debate, plans for a slide were ditched by a unanimous vote because one of the children, who used a wheelchair, wouldn't be able to use it. Undaunted, they opted for an adapted swing set instead. One of their grandparents told me a few years later there had been no damage or graffiti at all to the swings, in contrast to the other play equipment. 'It's theirs', she said, 'and they own it.'

There is a campaign running in Britain for a Community Power Act that would enshrine in law the right to be consulted, to co-produce services and participate in budgeting. It takes inspiration from trials in participatory budgeting across the UK, which discovered that involving people in decisions about how their money is spent leads to significantly better decisions, is more trusted and considered more legitimate than decisions taken without people.[16] It has also prompted decision makers to become more agile, changing and evolving their ways of thinking to make things work for most people.[17] In Madrid, communities have taken it upon themselves to do this, reclaiming abandoned public spaces and using online networks to develop them – the people of the city coming together to write the story of their own future.[18] What unites all of these different groups is the recognition that if people drive outcomes and share in decision making, they make better decisions and those decisions last.

TILTING THE BALANCE

Who owns Britain? I would tell you the answer but, incredibly, nobody really knows.

Visiting Burnley recently, the names of two landlords came up constantly. They lived in London but had bought up vast numbers of houses that had been left to go to rack and ruin. The tenants were stranded in appalling, unfit accommodation which blighted many streets. Burnley is a Northern town with so much going for it, including a rich, active civil society and leaders in business and politics who live locally and show leadership nationally. But they were powerless to stop it.

This is a common story across Britain but one that is seldom told. In every part of our country, people have bought up land and buildings in large swathes, extracted wealth and left us to deal with the consequences.

In my constituency, there is a former pit village. At its centre stands a small row of terraced houses, home to a chip shop, a launderette, a café and a pie shop. Behind them is the local library, which still opens for a few hours a week after it was saved from closure by local volunteers. Just down the road there is a newsagent, a village school, a small Co-op, a Royal British Legion and a curry house. This is the centre of the village. A few years ago, the owner of one of the businesses rang me to say they were all facing a rent increase which none of them could afford. Their landlord, who lived in London, was unresponsive until I got involved. How can it be right that someone on the other side of the country – whether by intention or not – can put at risk the future of a whole village?

We need to tilt the balance back in favour of the makers, the carers and the creators so those who are in it for the long haul feel the system pulling in behind them. With some small changes we could.

We could close the loophole that allows landlords to charge inflated rates of housing benefit to house vulnerable tenants, without providing any support at all. This is the business model that has sustained a 62 per cent rise in this practice since 2016.[19]

We could end the arcane rules around compulsory purchase orders that allow investors to buy land, shopping centres, historic buildings and town centres and sit on them – watching prices rise as they decay, knowing eventually the council will have to buy them back at a premium. This archaic system allows speculators to extract land value at way above market rates, bleeding much needed money out of the system at a time when housebuilding is forecast to hit its lowest rate since the Second World War, a million people wait for a social home and homeownership is at its lowest level for a generation.

It costs the community too. I've lost track of the number of times people have asked me why land or a historic building has been left derelict, like the many mills across Lancashire – visible symbols of our contribution to the country's history, which have become a visible symbol of decay and decline. These buildings matter. They are part of our heritage and define who we are.

The environmental campaigner and author, Guy Shrubsole, has documented who owns land in England and Wales, and it isn't us.[20] His painstaking research led him to estimate that 30 per cent of all land is in the hands of the aristocracy and gentry, 18 per cent is owned by corporations and 17 per cent is owned by oligarchs and city bankers. Only 8.5 per cent is owned by the public sector and a whopping 17 per cent is unaccounted for. And it's getting worse.

The Centre for Public Data has documented how the number of homes in England and Wales owned by overseas buyers has tripled in the last decade.[21] It took a war in Ukraine to persuade the Government that those who seek to own our assets should at least have to tell us who they are. A long-promised 'register of overseas entities' will require those who wish to own UK land to identify their beneficial (actual) owners and register them. Still, now, not all beneficial owners must register, and information about who owns Britain isn't freely available. Surely it's a fairly basic principle that people should have the right to know who owns their town, village or city?

When I tried to find out who owns Wigan I discovered much of the information was not available without paying a fee and, like elsewhere, that much of our land and buildings which I had assumed were held in common were owned by private investors, many of them registered to tax havens overseas.

The privatisation of public spaces affects us all, but it affects some people to the point of inhumanity. Take this example from a *Guardian* investigation in 2017: 'I'm allowed to lie down on the grass, but not to close my eyes,' one homeless man, who goes by the moniker Yankee Dan, said at the recently opened Pancras Square, part of the pseudo-public King's Cross Estate. 'I tried to take a nap the other morning, just for an hour or two, and every time my eyes began to shut I was woken up by security guards.' Another homeless man at King's Cross, who did not wish to be identified, said that it was those on the margins of the society that came up hardest against the hidden rules and borders of the site. 'To the ordinary person, there's no distinction between here and there,' he said, pointing first at a public pavement by the taxi rank, and then at a privately owned road that leads north towards

Granary Square. 'To me, the difference is everything, because I'm not the sort of person they want over there.'[22]

The insidious rise of pseudo-public space is the result of Government demonstrably not doing its job. While it tries to micromanage millions of decisions that it has no clue about – which high street gets some money for a fresh lick of paint and which doesn't – it isn't even beginning to deal with the things that it should. Making sure we know who owns the public spaces, housing, historical buildings and social assets that make up a place and giving us the ability to take them back. Taking on the rentiers who extract from our communities. Tilting the balance of power back to people who are building, investing and creating.

Too often they are the last to be heard, not just locally but across every part of the public realm. There are ways to fix this. Replacing the House of Lords, long considered an anachronism in a democracy and mired in allegations of cronyism, with a territorial senate would bring the UK into line with most modern democracies and guarantee a voice to places that are currently sidelined.[23] Extending the voting franchise to sixteen- and seventeen-year-olds would at least give politicians pause for thought before they took the axe to programmes like the Education Maintenance Allowance, abolished in one ministerial meeting without reference to Parliament or to people. Every time we've extended the franchise it's enriched our debate. Surely in a democracy the question we should start with is not why, but why not?

We need more voices in politics, and nowhere more so than the media.

Three companies dominate more than 80 per cent of the British newspaper market: Reach PLC, News UK and DMG Media.[24] And an article in a national magazine last year posed the question: 'Four men own Britain's news media. Is that a problem for democracy?'[25] It went on to highlight that 75 per cent of national newspaper circulation is controlled by four families headed by powerful men: Viscount Rothermere, Rupert Murdoch, Evgeny Lebedev and Frederick Barclay.

The Leveson Report, set up in the wake of the phone hacking scandal in 2011, the Media Reform Coalition and the Cairncross Review have made a raft of proposals to ensure plurality in the media and defend independent journalism. What is clear through all of these reports is that high-quality public interest journalism matters and it is under threat. 'Given the evidence of a market failure in the supply of public-interest news', Cairncross writes, 'public intervention may be the only remedy.'[26]

Government, though, has been slow to respond. Pressure has been building for a decade to take seriously abuses of power, lack of regulation and reliance on algorithms in the online world where a handful of men own powerful platforms like Facebook and Twitter. This is the problem in reverse. In newspapers the owners can act as gatekeepers, narrowing and determining the range of views that are heard. Online everyone is heard, regardless of their impact, and that in turn silences others. I have lost count of the number of young girls telling me they aren't on social media because of the abuse, the predators, the sexism and racism they have to deal with alone. If it happened on the street, in theory, they could call the police. If it happens on social media, they are told to report it to the private company who decide whether it breaches their policies. The government has left it to the private realm to police, regulate and monitor the online world, so some people are heard and others are silenced.

It took five years from the publication of government proposals to get legislation to tackle this in front of MPs. The Online Safety Bill has been beset with problems and is taking years to progress through Parliament. Meanwhile, others have stepped into the breach. The group Stop Funding Hate has done incredible work informing companies that their advertising budgets are being used to help fund hate-filled, racist sites online. Many of them were previously unaware and have responded by taking action to withdraw their advertising (and with them the revenues) from those sites. They are stepping up, but where is our Government?

Meanwhile, free and reliable news sources are under threat. The BBC World Service is a trusted source of news in many parts of the world where the only alternative is state propaganda – a lifeline for many living under authoritarian rule. But uncertainty over the licence fee and pressure from the UK Government to make more use of commercial revenue streams has created real pressure on the service. It has coincided with the biggest growth in media reach from authoritarian states like China, Russia and Iran, who invest heavily in global news to increase their influence around the world.[27] The balance is tilted in their favour.

THE INTERNATIONAL SCENE

The global sphere is arguably where national governments matter most, where so many local problems – fake news, fraud, football ownership and flooding – must be solved. From climate change and global pandemics to global financial regulation and the use and abuse of new technology, there is not a single global challenge that can be solved by one nation working alone.

Throughout the time I served as shadow foreign secretary, the power imbalance was clear. Big money lobbyists have power, information and the time to devote to influencing decisions. While journalists do a great deal to uncover the detail of those closed deals, too little effort is made by politicians to communicate with and understand the concerns and needs of the electorate. This is my failing too. It was 2015, five years into my time as Wigan's MP, before I first discussed our membership of the EU with my constituents at a public meeting. In the absence of any meaningful discussion, too often we take the wrong cues entirely from the public.

This is true when it comes to our habit of treating climate change as an elite concern, instead of something that deeply affects families and businesses whose homes are now too often underwater or swelteringly hot. People may be turned off by climate advocates who block motorways or disrupt public transport, but they are four-square behind environmentalists like David Attenborough. It was this same gulf that led many politicians to see the vote to leave the EU as a vote against international cooperation without stopping to ask how that could possibly be the prevailing sentiment in towns that, within living memory, powered the world through the mines, mills, steelworks and factories. Even now, we have a government that is pursuing ever more outlandish measures to shut out refugees even when it is clear that the public is far ahead of its government in its desire to help those fleeing war in Ukraine.

The institutions we have feel remote and unaccountable because too often they are. This, I believe, was a major factor in driving the vote to leave the EU in Britain in 2016. It gives succour to the voices calling for us to turn inward. Just as 'America First' and 'Make America Great Again' have found resonance with so many in the US, there are those in the UK who maintain that a retreat into narrow nationalism will help resolve the issues we face.

In recent years the debate has been framed into a series of false binaries – defend the status quo or retreat from the world – and we have not challenged them. Instead, we have rushed headlong into the trap. Witness Theresa May in a speech to the Conservative Party Conference in 2016: 'If you are a citizen of the world, you are a citizen of nowhere.' Internationalism has become associated with membership of the global liberal elite. You can either be for your country or for the world.

The global institutions we need are now in real danger. Yes, they are under attack from those who seek to sow division to further their own agenda. But they are also undermined by an unwillingness or inability to reassert the primacy of people over profit, to cooperate to solve climate change, to pull together to safeguard our energy supplies in the face of Russian aggression, and to stop a race to the bottom of the good wages and security at work that form the basis of a decent, dignified life.

This is a problem that democratic governments are at last starting to wake up to. The Biden administration has put consent at the centre of its approach to foreign policy. At its heart is the recognition that foreign policy is domestic and the global is local. Or, as C.L.R. James put it, 'genuine internationalism must be based on the national scene'.

In his first major speech as secretary of state, Anthony Blinken said: 'I know that foreign policy can sometimes feel disconnected from our daily lives. It's either all about major threats – like pandemics, terrorism – or it fades from view. That's in part because it's often about people and events on the other side of the world, and it's about things you don't see – like crises stopped before they start, or negotiations that happen out of sight.

'But it's also because those of us who conduct foreign policy haven't always done a good job connecting it to the needs and aspirations of the American people. As a result, for some time now Americans have been asking tough but fair questions about what we're doing, how we're leading – indeed, whether we should be leading at all.

'With this in mind, we've set the foreign policy priorities for the Biden administration by asking a few simple questions. What will our foreign policy mean for American workers and their families? What do we need to do around the world to make us stronger here at home? And what do we need to do at home to make us stronger in the world?'[28]

I believe Britain could be stronger at home if we pursued a foreign policy that defends the interests of people across our four nations; a foreign policy that doesn't pander to a US government that imposes shattering tariffs on the Scotch Whisky industry but stands up to it; that doesn't celebrate a paper-thin Brexit agreement that threatens the Welsh farming industry but fights for better; that works with allies to stop jobs being offshored to China and India in a race to the bottom for workers there and here; and one that treats the Good Friday Agreement as an essential plank of the security of the people of Northern Ireland – an article of faith, not a bargaining chip. The failures of our actions abroad have slowly, little by little, undermined support for the UK in each of the four nations, straining at the invisible chain that binds our nations together. No wonder people are losing faith if their government isn't doing its job.

So we need to reset our approach, taking the health of our children, the strength of our communities, the dignity of our workforce and the security of our nation as the benchmark of our success abroad.

We should make national security our top priority; standing with NATO allies; forging stronger alliances with the US and Five Eyes intelligence alliance; deepening cooperation in the Indo-Pacific; and repairing a needlessly antagonistic relationship with our closest neighbours. How to achieve it? We must restore Britain's reputation as a consistent, reliable partner and do the heavy lifting needed to reinvest in our relationships across the world.

Close bilateral relations with European countries are enhanced by a constructive relationship with the EU itself. They must respect our decision to stand outside of the EU, just as we must respect the importance of the European project to our friends and neighbours. But from sanctions and trade to financial regulation and climate change the EU is an important partner and we should seek creative ways to work together.

Britain was one of the founding partners of NATO. We need to rebuild our institutions so they can succeed in these stormy and uncertain times. We should breathe new life into multilateral institutions, rejecting the idea that alliances can be purely transactional. They are built on solidarity and they survive only if they can pass that test.

Winston Churchill once said Britain stands at the centre of three majestic circles, 'at the very point of junction, and here in this Island … we have the opportunity of joining them all together',[29] able to exert influence in the world through strong and mutually reinforcing relationships with Europe, the USA and the Commonwealth. But too often our relationship with the world is founded on nostalgia. We should be working towards the future with those countries, to build a fairer global economy and develop clean energy to create jobs in places that once powered the world and will do so again.

Our partnership with the United States matters beyond vague talk about the historic special relationship. Both Wall Street and the City of London have an important role to play in safeguarding our national security. These are the places where dirty money from authoritarian regimes finds its home. The former FBI special agent Bob Levinson told the journalist Catherine Belton: 'Russian organised crime leaders, their members, their associates are moving into Western Europe, they are purchasing property, they are establishing bank accounts, they're establishing companies, they're weaving themselves into the fabric of society and by the time that Europe develops an awareness it's going to be too late.' Belton's extraordinary book, *Putin's People*, was published in 2020,[30] but she was warning of the growing influence of Russia on the UK many years before the invasion of Ukraine. Action to clean up the flows of ill-gotten capital into the City of London, safeguard our energy supplies and social assets (like football clubs), and defend the UK from cyber-attack have all been shamefully neglected in recent years. For both the US and UK they must now be a priority.

The global race to determine who owns space has gathered pace in recent years with India, China, Russia and the United States all trying to lay claim to the stratosphere. It would be a significant prize, gifting control over the satellite technology that governs global communications, early warning systems for floods and tsunamis and much else besides. We should take our global responsibilities to defend these spaces to be used for the common good as seriously as we should take the defence of public spaces here on earth.

We should reset the approach of the last forty years and take long-overdue domestic and international action to rebuild the economic security of Britain's people and the places we call home. We have focused on the potential for China to become the dominant global political power, but we have paid far too little attention to the consequences of China's economic model for the British people – a model which relies on low working standards, poor wages and unfair trade practices to drive growth. This has to change.

We need a new economic statecraft to help bridge the divide between the global and the local, working with trade unions and like-minded governments to defend working people the world over from the race to the bottom and levelling the playing field for those incredible bricks and mortar businesses who are rooted in our communities and invest in our people. British companies do not operate on a level playing field – limited protections against practices like Chinese steel 'dumping' flood the global market with cheap goods and constantly threaten UK industry and jobs. Even now, those protections are under threat of being watered down.[31] Instead we should build a trade policy fit for the twenty-first century, prioritising fairness as well as market access, protecting the environment, and championing labour rights from Bolton to Bangalore. Through all of this we should make environmental security our priority. Climate change threatens the future of our planet but it also directly affects the lives and prosperity of working-class people right now. It is a central element of the pursuit of social justice, not an addendum to it.

Is it even possible to build a foreign policy *with* the people? Some say not. But it has been done before. A century ago, the League of Nations, an organisation for international cooperation, was formed, and with it the League of Nations Union. At its peak, the British branch had over 400,000 members: people committed to the ideals of peace, international justice and collective security. The League had many flaws. It was dominated by the middle class; it failed to connect with the networks already established by workers and trade unionists across the country; and ultimately it did not survive. But it was a reminder that throughout history people have easily been able to connect the global and the local, not just after an earth-shattering war, but in times of peace.

In the early part of the last century, anti-colonialist movements made empires crumble. In the 1960s civil rights movements went on the march, blazing a trail across the world. Still now, the trade union movement in Britain devotes considerable energy and resources to standing with counterparts across the world to end the race to the bottom. And one of the first causes I ever took up as an MP was the case of Trafigura, a company that had dumped toxic waste in the Côte d'Ivoire with immense harm to people and planet. Environmentalists like Greenpeace knew that to win anywhere you have to win everywhere and it was their work with Amnesty International that forced the issue onto the global agenda and led to a successful legal action in the UK courts.[32] These are the sorts of people who are found in every generation. What is the history of foreign policy if not the history of people driving and shaping the world they live in?

That foreign policy is treated as an elite concern is not inevitable. Sophia Gaston from the British Foreign Policy Group has documented how deeply the British public recognises that the lives we live are shaped in the world beyond our waters.[33] She has suggested a whole range of ways to ground foreign policy in public consent: openness about what we are trying to achieve and the principles and values that form the ethical foundation of our approach; a values test that allows people to better judge the actions of their government; and what Jonathan Gilmore calls a 'public diplomacy' programme to sit alongside foreign diplomacy, to articulate to the people what is being done in their name. Maybe it is the area of politics that is hardest to ground in the interests and needs of the people – but it is where it most matters.

A MORE COMPLETE DEMOCRACY

There's much to appreciate about the British Parliament. For all the public perception and commentary about MPs, most are there to do a decent job and make a contribution. And in the bill committees and meeting rooms that are unseen by the public, they do quietly make a difference. I often wish people could see more of that. In adversity, people from all sides can rally around, offering valuable support to women who often bear the brunt of the worst abuse in politics. But for the most part I find its atmosphere and traditions stuffy, stifling and averse to change, no matter how unsustainable the status quo. The building is steeped in status and class and the culture is utterly obsessed with who is 'up' and who is 'down'. It's easy to get lost in it.

But the terrace of the House of Commons is the most awesome place. The river Thames opens up in front of you, the imposing gothic architecture falls away behind. In the centre of one of the busiest cities on earth it's a quiet place where I sometimes go to breathe and remember that Parliament isn't a job, it's a megaphone through which you can make sure people are heard who otherwise would be silenced.

On one particular day in 2010 I caught Tony Benn's eye. He was sitting alone just a few tables away and wandered over to have a chat. I barely knew him, but that never stopped him. Lots that he said has stuck with me. He famously (and often) repeated that there were five questions that ought to be asked of anyone in power: 'What power have you got? Where did you get it from? In whose interests do you use it? To whom are you accountable? And how do we get rid of you?' He would stress the final question with a mischievous grin. It was, I think, his favourite of them all. 'Anyone who cannot answer the last of those questions', he said 'does not live in a democratic system ... Only democracy gives us that right. That is why no one with power likes democracy. And that is why every generation must struggle to win it and keep it – including you and me, here and now.'

I don't think it is true that no one with power likes democracy. There are many of us in politics who love a good debate, even if we come off worse from it. I've always felt we learn deeper lessons when we lose the argument. And often we change our minds through the fire of those debates. But the system doesn't reward that. Instead, we're depicted as having been 'humiliated', 'slammed', 'flip-flopped' or 'U-turned'.

There can be solace in changing your mind. When I worked with child refugees, we were constantly battling immigration officers who were sanctioned to use what were appalling practices: using force to get families to board planes; separating mothers from their children in immigration detention centres; and, in one of the worst cases I've ever seen, hand-cuffing a teenage girl who had attempted suicide. So those of us who advocated for those children had a dim view of most UK border agency officials. But in 2008 the then children's secretary, Ed Balls, agreed enough was enough and brought migrant children under the remit of Children Act laws, creating, for the first time, a counter-balance to the brutality of the immigration system and recognising that these children should have some protection in law. Shortly afterwards I went to deliver training about working with vulnerable children for those very same immigration officials and I was bowled over by the enthusiasm and the relief. They were more than willing to be challenged on their assumptions and openly apologetic about the times they felt they'd got it wrong. Finally, they felt they had permission to do the right thing.

But I've also seen how seldom an openness, a willingness to engage, permeates the institutions we have built, especially those state-based institutions that are often the only safeguard for people who need them. The culture is often one that puts the institution first and the people last – defensive and heavy-handed. I've seen this most starkly in the work I've done with child abuse survivors over the last two decades. Even now, too many institutions close ranks to protect themselves when faced with serious allegations. Often fearful of opening themselves up to compensation claims, they compound the original harm, leaving children still at risk of harm and further damaging those who have bravely spoken up. Good government opens up choices and chances. Bad government can restrict them.

PRESS 1 AND HOPE FOR THE BEST

Political institutions belong to the people, but so often it doesn't feel like it. Too many people's experience of government is of an entity that does things to people, not with them: remote, unaccountable and monolithic. And illiberal states that do things to people, that stop them living larger, richer lives, command no legitimacy. The mark of any decent government, and functioning institutions, is a willingness to be challenged. But anyone who has had an overpayment notice for tax credits, appealed an asylum decision, or tried to question an academy or free school about its admission policies will tell you this is not just hard but is getting harder.

Systems should be flexible and human – take the social security system, which is built on huge contracts awarded to a handful of major companies who often commission local providers, colleges, charities, local businesses and community groups to do, on a shoestring, what only we know needs to be done. Between 2010 and 2015 a string of failures led to a reassessment of these contracts but in 2016 an undercover investigation by Channel 4's *Dispatches* programme revealed that the £140 million scheme run by CAPITA to assess whether people needed additional help because of disability found assessors were given just twenty days' training, completed reports about people before even assessing them and were warned if they didn't get through assessments quickly they would be financially penalised.[34]

Despite the anger, by 2022 little had changed. The Restart scheme which was set up to help long-term unemployed people back to work cost £2.9 billion but the companies who were contracted, including Serco, Maximus and G4S, have so far only helped 7 per cent of the people on it to find work.[35] The types of jobs in an area, local health challenges, transport problems, and culture all affect decisions about how to best support people who are trying to get back into work. They are things that are usually simply not understood by people hundreds of miles away where it is easier to see targets than people. While they dictate the system, those on the ground lack the flexibility to respond to changing needs. I've lost count of the number of people who have been through my constituency surgery over the last decade who knew what help they needed but couldn't get it because the system was too rigid.

A handful of major companies are able to extract profit for this 'service' and the government gets a problem off its desk, claiming victory for reducing the number of benefit claimants – even if it doesn't get people into work, it gets them out of the system. In 2019 I proposed that those who had been through this system should be put in charge of redesigning it, otherwise, those who lose are the people who need work, and the communities they live in. This theme has gained traction through champions like Vicky Foxcroft, Labour's disability spokesperson who recently said 'society will benefit from a system co-produced by disabled people, that treats all people with dignity.'

Systems should be accountable – it should be clear who is in charge of decision making and provide clear mechanisms to hold them to account. But the architecture for this has been stripped away over the last decade. Fees to access employment tribunal fees have shut many people out from justice. Appeal rights for asylum seekers and benefit claimants have been restricted, as has the right to ask courts for a review of decisions that might have been unlawful. The abolition of legal aid removed, with one stroke, the housing and employment rights that had been fought for and won over a century. At worst, I have seen heartbroken mothers standing in court trying to defend their right to see their children after a divorce without any understanding of how to do so because of the absence of legal help. What use are rights without the means to enforce them?

Systems should be straightforward and clear. This is where I think the tax credit system has taken a wrong turn. It was a smart scheme, devised by smart people, and provides a far more efficient way to get help to the people who most need it than the rises in personal allowance favoured by the Tories, which do nothing for the very poorest, while helping the wealthiest too. But the complexity of the process means that payments are often inaccurate, and when it goes wrong those in need pay the price. Everybody in the system dreads the word 'overpayment'. It is frightening to get a computer-generated letter, in inhuman language, telling you to repay large sums of money you cannot afford, when your family's future rests on resolving it and the only option to do so is an automated helpline. When the only option is to press 1 and hope for the best, that is not the mark of a state that respects and supports its people.

CHECKS AND BALANCES

But the state is just one part of a bigger democratic ecosystem – a free media, independent judiciary and free elections – that have all been under attack in recent years. This includes that most important of spaces that exists between states and markets, neglected by political parties of all colours for too long – civil society.

The charities, voluntary groups, cooperatives and trade unions who make up civil society are essential in a democracy but they too are under attack. The rights of workers to self-organise and show solidarity with others were eroded in the 1980s and have never been restored. Trade unions still have large memberships but they have dwindled over time. While some have been beset by the same problems as the institutions they are supposed to hold accountable – charges of corruption and discriminatory practices have been upheld against two major unions in recent years – their workplace representatives and national officers have quietly provided an essential ballast against state and market power over that time. I have worked with countless such trade unionists who are the last and only hope against the abuse and mistreatment of disabled people, the elderly and families. Whether it's defending pay and pensions, health and safety, or standing against 'fire and rehire' or taking on British Gas, without the collective action of the nation's workers we would be in a far worse place.

The charity sector hasn't been immune from its own problems. I worked in what is known as the 'third sector' for a decade and saw how a desire to be close to government had left some big charities too reliant on government contracts and less willing to challenge. The higher I got in the charity world, the less likely I was to see people who looked like the people we existed for. In recent years a handful of those leaders have been exposed for excessive salaries and perpetuating the sort of discrimination charities were founded to fight.

One example of this during my time at The Children's Society involved a donation made to us by BrightHouse, a credit agency who provide furniture upfront but charge high interest rates on the loan. During that time predatory loan sharks were blighting the lives of many of the families we worked with. So when we opposed the decision to take the money, it was a mark of a good organisation that our Chief Executive, Bob Reitemeier, listened, agreed, and the money was returned. He was, like many charity leaders, prepared to do extraordinary things and take big risks to help the children who needed us. We set up a base in the family wing of Yarl's Wood Immigration Detention Centre and, by showing the truth of what was happening to families there, campaigned (successfully) to close it down. We dug into our charity reserves to give grants to families who were told they were in the UK illegally, some of whom were literally starving. We were threatened by the Home Office, but we did it anyway. It was the first time the organisation had given out direct grants to families since the Miners' Strike. 'It has to be cash', our (then) in-house vicar Nigel Asbridge told the trustees, 'because what do we stand for if not dignity?'

Charities hold power to account. It is why, when the Charities minister told charities to stop lobbying government and 'stick to their knitting', those charity representatives who reacted with fury were right.[36] Charities don't just have the right, they have a duty to speak up for the people they represent. That is why the Lobbying Act passed in 2014, which restricts their ability to speak out, controlling what they can say and do publicly in the twelve-month run-up to elections, is an affront not just to charities but to all of us.[37]

For as long as it has existed, people have known that democracy is not without its limitations and its flaws. But it was Alexis De Tocqueville, writing at the birth of American democracy, who coined the phrase 'the tyranny of the majority'. Whether it's homeless teenagers demonised by sections of the media or asylum-seeking children shunned by the government, for minorities democracy is not always a comfortable experience.

The state, private companies, the media, sections of the public and political parties can trample over minority rights. Guarding against this is part of what politics is for, but when it fails, civil society is the safety valve. It is, as Maurice Glasman says, the defender of reciprocity and relationships.

It isn't just minorities who should care about this. We all should, as Michael Walzer explains in his essay *The Historical Task of the Left in the Present Period*: 'What the most vulnerable people need right now is the protection afforded by a strong constitutionalism. The defense of civil liberties and civil rights in the name of the constitution – this is a centrist politics ... Never think that "the blood-dimmed tide" is a threat only to immigrants and minorities. It is a threat to all of us ... We all need constitutional protection; we all need a center that holds. We have to stand in the center and on the left at the same time. That may be complicated, but it is our historical task.'[38]

We should recognise the importance of civil society again, nurture it, defend and protect it. And we should learn from it.

WITH THE PEOPLE

For all our enthusiasm for the state, the Labour Party was born out of civil society. The Great Dock Strike of 1889 was an uprising sparked by the low pay, poor working conditions and appalling living standards London dockers were forced to endure. It led to the formation of the Dockers' Union, which later became the Transport and General Workers' Union and is now Unite. This was working people standing together, fighting together and winning together. As Maurice Glasman says: 'it was led by the people themselves. You can't change the world at all unless you are prepared to open yourselves to others, to be in relationship with others, and then, from being faithful to your own tradition, open up to the goodness in other traditions to build an association and a greater bond. And this, extraordinarily, was how my party, the Labour Party, was born. But if you tell the story in the Labour Party today, no-one even remembers it. They say we were founded to create equality and justice and diversity and accessibility and inclusivity. This really wasn't the language of the dockers during the dock strike. Their language was "brotherhood", "solidarity", "vocation" ... Alone in Europe, the labour movement in this country was not divided along religious lines nor between religious and secular, but was a broad based, quite deeply conservative movement that was attached to family, place and the representation of labour interests ... There is a magnificent inheritance that we can take from this. First of all, that it's not a fantasy nor even idealistic but a matter of necessity that we must trust each other, that we must find a way of working together and acting together, not for our individual good alone but for a common good. It should aim to build the power of people so that they can have a say, not a dominant say, but a voice in the governance of politics and the governance of the economy.'[39]

I believe a state that can stand in defence of equality, justice, diversity, accessibility and inclusivity is an unequivocally good thing. But I think Maurice Glasman is right when he points to something that has been lost: the argument that the state, markets and society should explicitly support and defend the common good. And I think we need to reclaim this tradition to put it at the heart of how we govern. Liberalising the state so it is no longer other to us, but among us. Using with greater care the tools that so easily divide us from one another, like referendums, and embracing different ways of bringing us together, like citizens assemblies which bring more voices into the conversation. This is the way to bolster and sustain the leaders we need – those that can embrace the complexity that politics too often cannot accommodate.

THIS IS WHAT A LEADER LOOKS LIKE

In 2019 a young man walked up to the door of a mosque in Christchurch, New Zealand, with an assault rifle visible in his hands. The elderly Afghan man who stood at the door greeted him with the words, 'Hello brother'. Moments later the gunman opened fire. People from across the world were gathered in the mosque for prayer, and fifty-one of them were killed. It was a tragedy that reverberated around the world.

When the then Prime Minister Jacinda Ardern arrived in Christchurch wearing a black headscarf, the swiftness of the visit and meaning of the gesture were clearly appreciated. But when she reached forward to hug the victims, telling reporters 'they are us', the images resonated around the world. Human, warm, empathetic and responsive – unafraid to wear her heart on her sleeve – in that moment Jacinda Ardern was everything people believe politics is not.

There are leaders who have channelled 'human' qualities in modern times – many of them on the populist right. They put their personality on display but display their humanity only in order to dehumanise others. That is maybe why Ardern stands out, because she showed not just a human side but genuine humanity. Martin Luther King once said 'a genuine leader is not a searcher for consensus but a moulder of consensus'.

Why don't we have more of these types of leaders? In her book, *Why We Get the Wrong Politicians*,[40] the journalist Isabel Hardman highlights the path to power, which often involves patronage, money or being from the 'right' class, gender or race. Responding to the debate that Hardman started, my friend Jess Phillips, the MP for Birmingham Yardley, pinpointed the culture: 'These times of pearl-clutching, hero worship and searing hatred don't lend themselves to people who are willing to present themselves in shades of grey, when people seek black and white. We are seldom rewarded for saying "it's complicated".'[41]

But it is. And we need those sorts of leaders. In his book, *The Myth of the Strong Leader*,[42] Archie Brown rates among the best leaders those who are collegiate, conciliatory, and willing to delegate. He cites Harry Truman in the United States, a reluctant leader, as the Platonic ideal – one who didn't seek power and can therefore be entrusted with it. 'It was characteristic of Truman's style', he writes 'that the most outstanding foreign policy achievement of his presidency is known as the Marshall Plan, not the Truman Plan.' He also singles out Clement Attlee, whose cabinet was made up of some of the giants of their century. Bevan. Bevin. Cripps. Gaitskell. Wilson. Could this be because, just as a state which dwarfs its people will find with small men no great thing can be achieved, so too will a leader who dwarfs her (or more often his) cabinet?

Attlee is unusual. Because, as Archie Brown shows, those who are ranked best amongst the public are usually those considered 'strong'. The tough, decisive leader who takes all the decisions themselves wins the popular contest, while (he argues) good leaders have rarely fitted this mould. It is an important lesson that we need to rethink our own ideas about what leaders look like. Maybe it's already happening. As one magazine wrote following Ardern's visit to Christchurch, 'This is what a leader looks like.'

LIFE IS COMPLICATED

For me, politics is about negotiating shared challenges in the interests of the many. It is rarely straightforward. Just like life, it requires give and take, compromise and the ability to change your mind. Politics is complicated because life is complicated. We need a political system that doesn't try to erase that complexity and messiness at the heart of the human condition but embraces it and finds the way through.

Maybe it's because of my family background that spans Liberalism and Marxism and much in between – with immediate family from different cultures, nations and traditions – that I believe this complexity, difference and messiness is what fuels us.

In 2008 Beijing hosted the Olympics. The opening ceremony is memorable for many things, not least the child who sang like an angel but was later revealed to have been asked to mime. The child with the voice was told her face didn't fit.[43] But this was clearly a nation on the march – extending its economic and political power across the world – and this was the moment to shine. The image that was beamed into homes across the world was of a flawless, powerful, uniform nation; at its centre, the earth-shattering sound of 2,008 people in the year 2008 drumming to one beat.

But the exiled Chinese artist Ai Weiwei, who designed the centrepiece of that ceremony – the Bird's Nest – later withdrew his support. This was a nation projecting power because it had to. Four years later, Danny Boyle's London 2012 opening ceremony could not have been a bigger contrast.

'This was about Great Britain,' Ai Weiwei wrote afterwards, 'the land, the women, the machinery ... it didn't pretend it was trying to have global appeal. Because Great Britain has self-confidence, it doesn't need a monumental Olympics. It celebrated everyone,' he wrote, from 'the Queen to the nurse.'[44]

A country that can be honest about its past in all its vibrant, messy complexity and take pride in its successes, that can celebrate the people who made us and make us still; that is able to say 'This is us. This is who we are' – that is a country that can forge a path onwards and help to light up the world. The people have got there. It's time for our politics to catch up.

7.

THE TILT

'Who in the world am I? Ah, that's the great puzzle.'
Lewis Carroll, *Alice in Wonderland*

The world is spinning on its axis, buffeting a country that is cast adrift. Much of the recent political turmoil has been an expression of wider malaise – a failure to adequately respond to a rapidly changing country in a rapidly changing world. During my lifetime we've seen the near end of industrialisation, the emancipation of women in the workplace, and the explosion of education in Britain and across the world.

The dominance of China has dislodged the world order. Supranational companies dwarf countries and can impose conditions, limitations and standards on people from afar. As I write, P&O Ferries, operating in Britain since the 1960s and owned by Dubai-based DP World since 2019, have sparked an outcry after telling 800 British workers they have been discarded for cheaper labour, with immediate effect, via video link. Did the company break the law? Almost certainly, admitted the CEO, 'but so what?'

For people and places alike – both winners and losers over recent decades – this isn't the end of history so much as the end of certainty.

We are in the midst of a technological revolution that, as James Burke predicted, has connected Manhattan to the Himalayas, enabling revolutions to rise and to fall at the touch of a button, sparking the rise of super-stellar cities that have pulled the rest of us into their orbit, at once connecting us and driving us further apart.

We are richer but more unequal, more interconnected but far more divided. Nothing encapsulates this better than COVID-19 and climate change, two unique global challenges that have pulled us apart even as they drive us together.

Now the race is on to own the next chapter – the era of security and resilience – to shorten supply chains, expand home-grown industries, especially in security critical areas like energy and telecoms and to equip young people to be able to stay and contribute, not just escape for a better life.

A reimagined economy demands a different sort of politics too, an end to the command and control politics that has characterized political leadership and leaders for a century, and a respect for all of our people and places – recognising that they have both a contribution to make to the future of our country and a right to a fair share in its success.

As the certainties of the past have crumbled we have clung to what we knew with a tighter and tighter grip. It is not working. As Khrushchev once wrote to Kennedy, 'The tighter we pull, the tighter the knot is tied.'

SHIFTING SANDS

I became the MP for Wigan in 2010, nearly two decades after the last mine had closed where once there had been 1000 pit shafts within a five-mile radius. It is an amazing town, full of entrepreneurs, talent and with good local leaders across politics, business, public services and civil society who are in it for the long haul. But blasted by the headwinds of the last forty years, the pace, scale and nature of change have stripped Wigan of its inheritance and of the future we once thought was ours, as it has for many such communities.

A proud, tight-knit, ambitious community has watched too many good jobs hived off to nearby cities and far-off lands, and with them young people, spending power, thriving high streets and our contribution to Britain – our place in the national story.

This clamour for change has been misinterpreted, sometimes wilfully, as a desire to turn the clock back to a time that no longer exists or to stop the world and get off. This couldn't be further from the truth.

The everyday pragmatism of the people I have represented for over a decade has helped me understand that the problem is not that the world has changed – it always has, and always will – but that as it has changed around us, we have stood still.

We haven't shaped the world. We've been thrown by it. We are stuck, unable to move forwards for lack of an idea of what we're moving towards, or how to make it happen. It has cost people and places in Britain dear: not just our jobs, our local economies and our social fabric but our place in an increasingly confused national story.

WHO IN THE WORLD ARE WE?

The EU Referendum landed in the midst of this, throwing out certainties and bringing to the fore questions about who we are, what we stand for, and whether in fact we can even stand together for anything.

At its peak, 60 per cent of people identified with the most extreme Leave or Remain position: 'a stronger association than any other political or value-based position', according to the anti-fascist group Hope Not Hate. The rise of these seemingly new divisions and attachments sparked an introspective, at times alarmist, debate about enduring, irreparable division. But as Hope Not Hate acknowledged, Brexit merely shone a spotlight on divisions that had been with us and growing for some time. These were 'the expression of conflicts that had been building in the electorate for decades', as Sobolewska and Ford put it in *Brexitland*, not their cause.[1]

And yet the debate it sparked about Britain and our place in the world divided us further still and ran us into the sand.

For some politicians, we are a small island nation who still find our identity through Empire – a country that once ruled the waves. For others we are a nation who found our place in the world and amplified our voice through our membership of the European Union. Outside of the EU, they ask, have we a hope?

On the face of it these are visions for Britain that are worlds apart. But look closer and the curious thing about both is how backward-looking and increasingly steeped in nostalgia they are. By presenting themselves as positive visions of the past they disguise that they are both deeply pessimistic views of Britain's future.

Perhaps because of my family history, I see things differently. Our relationship with the countries that once made up Britain's Empire and the nations that still comprise the EU may have been central to our past, but for both to remain central to our future we need a new approach. Now, long after the end of Empire and freshly out of the EU, we need to think harder about how to renew those relationships to help shape the world beyond our shores. The shockwaves caused by the scandalous treatment of the Windrush Generation convinced me that we can only do that if we're clear about who we are and what we stand for, at home and abroad.

So, as we look to the future, I think of the Manchester I grew up in: a city shaped by its people, who fought for change and were themselves changed by waves of immigration. People like my dad, who made his home in that great city in the 1980s. My favourite museum, the People's History Museum, tells the story of the pioneers who built and shaped that great city over centuries and always looked forwards to ask, 'Where next?'

Hope lies in each other and in the pragmatism of a public that has adapted and changed even as the systems that govern us haven't.

Far from being endlessly divided, 'the truth', say Sobolewska and Ford, 'is messier, but more hopeful'. Divisions might run deep, but most of us 'share a common vision for Britain as a responsive democracy that values the rights of its citizens and responds to their needs. While many find the vast demographic and social changes of recent decades disorientating and seek reassurance from their politicians in response, they also show a tremendous capacity to adapt.'[2]

Maybe it isn't Britain that is stuck. Maybe it's our politics. We have spent so long looking backwards and turning inwards that we neither control our own destiny nor shape the world beyond our shores. What is stopping us?

THE NORTH STAR

In the children's story *The Emperor's New Clothes*, a pompous Emperor commissions a suit of new clothes. The weavers pretend to weave him a suit of clothes that they say are so magnificent they are invisible only to those who are too stupid to see them. Not wanting to reveal his stupidity, the Emperor dons the 'suit' and parades through the streets stark naked. The crowds remain silent, unwilling to admit they cannot see it, until finally a child shouts out the truth and the spell is broken.

Participating in British politics sometimes feels like standing in that crowd, surrounded by intelligent people pulling 'levers with no strings attached', as the MP Jon Cruddas put it to me, acting the part of power brokers when power has long since moved elsewhere. Sometimes it has the unreal feeling of a charade about it. This is why, when the rush to attend Prime Minister's Questions begins on a Wednesday morning, almost without exception, I'm found heading in the other direction.

National government matters like never before. But increasingly the scale and speed of change are making demands of government it can no longer meet. Built in a different era, before the rise of global corporations, before mass education, before climate change, national government increasingly feels clunky and detached, trying to micro-manage millions of decisions it can't control, but unwilling or unable to clear the pitch for those who could.

This is what I think is at the heart of the feeling of malaise. Governments that lack a clear sense of what they are for, what we're collectively trying to achieve, and whose job it is to do it.

This stands in stark contrast to what I have seen in communities across Britain.

When Wigan Athletic collapsed, the whole community responded at speed to devastating, unexpected circumstances because everything was at stake. There is nothing romantic about this. It was a necessity not a choice. It wasn't always easy. Communities are complicated. People hold different views, and the differences could have derailed us. But they didn't, because in the end we knew what was at stake, what needed to be done, and we strove relentlessly towards it. We didn't need a focus group to tell us what to do. We saw our North Star and moved heaven and earth to reach it.

But the story of how we saved Wigan Athletic, like the residents of Perry Common who saved their estate, and the hospital workers who defended their jobs, wages and ideals – these stories are dwarfed by the stories of those who trod this path before us and were defeated in their aims. So often they were defeated because the power and resources they needed were denied to them by an overly centralised system and a national government that wasn't doing its job.

In part, this book is intended as a rallying cry that they must have the tools they need to rise to the scale of the challenge in front of them. So often, to pull off extraordinary feats in our communities we have to find ways to cheat the logic of the system. So why don't we change the system?

It is also a call to action, a statement that government has to change to allow change in the country. It must stop trying to do our job and start doing its own. To clear the pitch so that nobody can hoard money and power, by taking on big monopolies and breaking them up, working with other like-minded governments to do the same, and contributing to the institutions and culture that we need – that can bring us together, rather than break us apart – so we can build the future, from the ground up and put people who have skin in the game in charge of decisions.

THE ENEMY OF HUMANITY

If this sounds messy and complicated, it's because it is. From my early twenties as a young councillor in West London helping a community navigate shared challenges – from hot button issues like parking permits and proposed homeless shelters –

to my time as shadow foreign secretary sitting with Israeli and Palestinian politicians to discuss the shrinking prospects of peace, I have learnt that politics is complicated because life is complicated. Our inability to embrace and deal with difference in politics is the sign of a system creaking at the seams.

No one person has the monopoly on wisdom. Democracy is hard. But the airing of different points of view, the clash of ideas, leadership that can challenge and compromise, gives us better decisions. And anyway, when did the path of least resistance ever point towards progress?

We could use more institutions that help us do this right now. But too often the institutions we have, built in different times, are unfit for this stormy age, pulling us apart rather than bringing us together. Too often they feel other or alien to people. Big, remote and unresponsive. Pulling against us, rather than with us.

There is a rich seam of Labour thinking that has always stood against this tradition. It was Clement Attlee who said socialism is a more 'exacting creed' than its competitors, because it demands of us 'active, constant participation'. He understood that change which lasts is change that is built on consent. At times over the last century we have briefly forgotten this, but thankfully the public has not. The future will be negotiated, not imposed or announced from the centre.

In his speech to Parliament introducing the National Assistance Act, which would sweep away the workhouses that had come to characterise the inhumanity of Victorian Britain, Nye Bevan argued passionately that the newly formed care homes for older people must not become big faceless remote institutions. 'I have been cudgelling my brains to find a name for them', he said 'but it is very difficult.' In the end he declared we should not call them by a general name at all because 'bigness is the enemy of humanity'. Like Bevan's generation we find the answers to big universal questions lie in the local and particular – and we do have to find them.

Some seventy-five years later we badly need new institutions, like the citizens' assemblies that have been utilised in Ireland, Australia, Canada and the United States, to help us navigate difference and embrace complexity. During Brexit I was so struck by the difference between families who had voted different ways on Brexit but who had put aside those differences and moved on to a position of compromise, while politicians seemed unable to move forwards. Families navigate difference all the time. And though it isn't always easy we tend not to walk away. Why? Because we have a stake.

There is power in this. It is what spurs on communities, bound together by common goals and a shared stake, to make change when it seems altogether impossible. I've been an MP for twenty-one election cycles, and I have learnt that communities endure as governments come and go. Britain is made up of people who can endure and evolve, and who know instinctively that we achieve more by our common endeavour than we achieve alone. That is why politics must, above all, get comfortable with the messiness, complexity and diversity that is modern Britain.

In recent years the best expression of this I can find in politics is the Good Friday Agreement which was and remains an article of faith – for Labour and for me.

The beauty of the Good Friday Agreement was its recognition and embrace of multiple, overlapping identities. You could be British, Irish, Northern Irish, a combination or none at all. Identity is not a zero-sum game. I am proudly British, English and proud of my Indian heritage too. I'm fiercely Northern, a Mancunian by birth and a Wiganer by choice. Like most people, I see no contradiction in the many different strands that make me who I am.

A country that can be at ease with the multiple, overlapping identities of its citizens, and as a consequence can connect with people all over the world, that can accommodate different views and come to a common purpose for all its people, in all its places, not just some – that is a country that can rise to this moment.

The last forty years have brought enormous progress in education, healthcare and technology. All have taken great leaps forwards, but to what ends? That is for us to decide. If we chose to we could now 'do away with the greatest tragedy of our era. The centuries old waste of human talent,' as James Burke suggested, and build, together.

For all the distortion, the real history of Britain is one of waves of immigration that helped to shape the composition of our country and of quiet, pragmatic patriotism that has spurred us on to adapt and change. Our shared history has shone a light at home and helped us at our best moments to show that light in the world, working to change things for the better beyond our own shores. Moments of darkness force us to think, to learn, and propel us forwards – led by ordinary, extraordinary people, who have worked together across so many divides to write the story of Britain.

Britain evolves and so do we. This is why we must remember who we are, and can be: a country at ease with itself, which can find a place and a role for all of its people. A state that respects its people and hands the reins of power to communities who have a shared stake in our future is one that will succeed. We've done it before, at times in our history, and we've seen what it can achieve. In this moment where so much has broken, where nothing is certain, and where so much is at stake, hope burns brighter than ever in every corner of Britain. It's time to do it again.

ACKNOWLEDGEMENTS

To Ian Warren for the ideas, writing, inspiration and for buying the drinks when it all went wrong. Without you there would be no book.

Thanks to Jon Cruddas, Jonathan Rutherford, Marianne Sensier, Glen O'Hara. Anand Menon and countless others who have helped me to work through the ideas in this book. Special thanks to Will Jennings for warning me that writing a book was a very bad idea and to my editor Jon for persuading me otherwise. To Charlotte Warren for the cover advice, P&E for the encouragement, Charlotte Carpentier for the chats about French politics and to my family, for everything.

Most of all thank you to the incredible people in Wigan and across Britain who have opened up your homes and communities to me and convinced me that things can be different. This book is for you.

ENDNOTES

1. THE CHALLENGE

1. David Conn, 'Brutal and Bizarre: The Story of How Wigan Collapsed into Administration', *Guardian*, 2 July 2020: https://www.theguardian.com/football/2020/jul/02/story-of-how-wigan-collapsed-into-administration-au-yeung-investigation.

2. THE WORLD TRANSFORMED

1. World Bank Gender Data Portal: https://genderdata.worldbank.org/.
2. UN Women, 'Facts and Figures: Women's Leadership and Political Participation', 15 January 2021: https://www.unwomen.org/en/what-we-do/leadership-and-political-participation/facts-and-figures.
3. World Economic Forum, 'Global Gender Gap Report', n.d.: https://www3.weforum.org/docs/WEF_GGGR_2021.pdf; Glenn-Marie Lange, Quentin Wodon and Kevin Carey (eds), 'The Changing Wealth of Nations 2018: Building a Sustainable Future', The World Bank, 2018: https://openknowledge.worldbank.org/bitstream/handle/10986/29001/9781464810466.pdf?sequence=4&isAllowed=y.
4. Freedom House, 'New Report: The Global Decline in Democracy has Accelerated', 3 March 2021: https://freedomhouse.org/article/new-report-global-decline-democracy-has-accelerated; 'Globalisation and Autocracy are Locked Together. For How Much Longer?', *Economist*, 19 March 2022: https://www.economist.com/finance-and-economics/2022/03/19/globalisation-and-autocracy-are-locked-together-for-how-much-longer.

5. Eric Hobsbawm, *The Age of Extremes: The Short Twentieth Century*, 1914–1991, London: Michael Joseph, 1994.
6. Harold Evans, *The American Century*, New York: Alfred A. Knopf, 1998.
7. Danny Finkelstein, 'Are We Witnessing End of the American Era?', *The Times*, 8 April 2020: https://www.thetimes.co.uk/article/are-we-witnessing-end-of-the-american-era-bbqk3k99p.
8. The World Bank, 'The World Bank in China', 12 April 2022: http://www.worldbank.org/en/country/china/overview.
9. Kerry Brown, *The World According to Xi*, Bloomsbury, 2018.
10. Hobsbawm, *The Age of Extremes*.
11. Brown, *The World According to Xi*.
12. Address by Secretary General Dag Hammarskjöld at University of California Convocation, Berkeley, California, Thursday, 13 May 1954: https://digitallibrary.un.org/record/1291161?ln=en.
13. Shaun Walker, 'Coronavirus Diplomacy: How Russia, China and EU Vie to Win Over Serbia', *Guardian*, 13 April 2022: https://www.theguardian.com/world/2020/apr/13/coronavirus-diplomacy-how-russia-china-and-eu-vie-to-win-over-serbia.
14. António Guterres, 'Opening remarks at Nelson Mandela Lecture: "Tackling the Inequality Pandemic: A New Social Contract for a New Era"', United Nations, 18 July, 2020: https://www.un.org/sg/en/content/sg/speeches/2020-07-18/remarks-nelson-mandela-lecture-tackling-the-inequality-pandemic-new-social-contract-for-new-era.
15. Oliver J. Watson et al., 'Global Impact of the First Year of COVID-19 Vaccination: A Mathematical Modelling Study', 23 June 2022, *The Lancet*: https://www.thelancet.com/journals/laninf/article/PIIS1473-3099(22)00320-6/fulltext.
16. Mark Carney, 'Breaking the Tragedy of the Horizon – Climate Change and Financial Stability', Bank of England, 29 September 2015: https://www.bankofengland.co.uk/speech/2015/breaking-the-tragedy-of-the-horizon-climate-change-and-financial-stability.
17. Helen Thompson, Disorder: *Hard Times in the 21st Century*, Oxford: Oxford University Press, 2022.
18. 'The Urge to Protect: How Trade Restrictions are Being Used as a Tool to Protect Human Rights', *Economist*, 6 October 2021: https://www.economist.com/special-report/2021/10/06/the-urge-to-protect.
19. Uyghur Tribunal, 'UK Tribunal to Investigate China's Alleged Genocide and Crimes against Humanity against Uyghur, Kazakh and other Turkic Muslim Populations', n.d.: https://uyghurtribunal.com/.
20. Adrian Shahbaz and Allie Funk, 'Freedom on the Net 2019: The Crisis of Social Media', Freedom House, n.d.: https://www.

freedomonthenet.org/sites/default/files/2019-11/11042019_Report_
FH_FOTN_2019_final_Public_Download.pdf.
21. Lange, Wodon and Carey (eds), 'The Changing Wealth of Nations'.
22. Joseph E. Stiglitz, 'US Trade Deals were Designed to Serve
    Corporations at the Expense of Workers', CNBC, 21 April 2019:
    https://www.cnbc.com/2019/04/22/joseph-stiglitz-us-trade-deals-
    helped-corporations-and-hurt-workers.html.
23. Review of Thomas Piketty, *Capital in the Twenty-First Century*
    [translated by Arthur Goldhammer, Harvard University Press/
    Belknap Press], 15 April 2014: https://www.ft.com/
    content/0c6e9302-c3e2-11e3-a8e0-00144feabdc0.
24. Michael Young, *Small Man, Big World*.
25. Edward Helmore, 'G20 Leaders to Endorse Biden Proposal for
    Global Minimum Corporate Tax', *Guardian*, 30 October 2021:
    https://www.theguardian.com/world/2021/oct/30/g20-leaders-
    endorse-biden-global-minimum-corporate-tax.

3. POPULISM, PATRIOTISM AND POWER

1. James Slack, 'Enemies of the People: Fury Over "Out of Touch"
   Judges who have "Declared War on Democracy" by Defying
   17.4m Brexit Voters and who could trigger constitutional crisis',
   Daily Mail, 3 November 2016: https://www.dailymail.co.uk/news/
   article-3903436/Enemies-people-Fury-touch-judges-defied-17-4m-
   Brexit-voters-trigger-constitutional-crisis.html.
2. Jesse Norman, *The Big Society: The Anatomy of the New Politics*,
   Buckingham: University of Buckingham Press, 2010.
3. Will Jennings and Gerry Stoker, 'The Bifurcation of Politics: Two
   Englands', 17 March 2016, *Political Quarterly*, https://
   onlinelibrary.wiley.com/doi/abs/10.1111/1467-923X.12228.
4. 'Revealed: Trust in Politicians at Lowest Level on Record', IPPR, 5
   December 2021: https://www.ippr.org/news-and-media/press-
   releases/revealed-trust-in-politicians-at-lowest-level-on-record/.
5. Matt Bolton and Frederick Harry Pitts, *Corbynism: A Critical
   Approach*, Bingley: Emerald Publishing, 2018.
6. 'English Indices of Deprivation 2019: Research Report': https://
   www.gov.uk/government/publications/english-indices-of-
   deprivation-2019-research-report.
7. George Orwell, *The Lion and the Unicorn: Socialism and the
   English Genius*, London: Secker & Warburg, 1941.
8. Jonathan Freedland, 'Danny Boyle: champion of the people',
   Guardian, 9 March 2013: https://www.theguardian.com/film/2013/
   mar/09/danny-boyle-queen-olympics-film.
9. Peter Hain, *Back to the Future of Socialism*, Bristol: Policy Press,
   2015.

10. Ernest Hemingway, *To Have and Have Not*, New York: Charles Scribner's Sons, 1937.
11. 'England and Its Discontents', IPPR, 2012: https://www.ippr.org/publications/england-and-its-two-unions-the-anatomy-of-a-nation-and-its-discontents.
12. Dan Hodges, *Mail on Sunday*, 16 May 2021, https://www.dailymail.co.uk/debate/article-9583225/DAN-HODGES-Labour-cares-Palestinians-Red-Wall-voters.html.

4. A NATION OF WINNERS AND LOSERS

1. TUC, 'Gig Economy Workforce in England and Wales Has Almost Tripled in Last Five Years – New TUC Research', 5 November 2021: https://www.tuc.org.uk/news/gig-economy-workforce-england-and-wales-has-almost-tripled-last-five-years-new-tuc-research.
2. Louie Smith, 'Amazon Workers 'Treated like Slaves and Robots' as Ambulances Called to Centres 971 Times', *Mirror*, 23 November 2021: https://www.mirror.co.uk/news/uk-news/amazon-workers-treated-like-slaves-25531239.
3. Supreme Court, 'Uber BV and Others (Appellants) v Aslam and Others (Respondents)', 21–22 July 2020: https://www.supremecourt.uk/cases/uksc-2019-0029.html.
4. Nikki Pound, 'Record Wealth Inequality Shows Why Our Economy is Rigged against Working People', TUC, 6 December 2019: https://www.tuc.org.uk/blogs/record-wealth-inequality-shows-why-our-economy-rigged-against-working-people.
5. Tim Sharp, 'Fire and Rehire Tactics are Levelling Down Pay', TUC, 25 January 2021: https://www.tuc.org.uk/blogs/fire-and-rehire-tactics-are-levelling-down-pay.
6. Jack Dromey, 'Jayaben Desai Obituary', *Guardian*, 28 December 20210: https://www.theguardian.com/politics/2010/dec/28/jayaben-desai-obituary.
7. Kwasi Kwarteng, Priti Patel, Dominic Raab, Chris Skidmore and Liz Truss, *Britannia Unchained: Global Lessons for Growth and Prosperity*, London: Palgrave Macmillan, 2012.
8. Matthew Keep, 'Country and Regional Public Sector Finances', House of Commons Library, 20 January 2020: https://commonslibrary.parliament.uk/research-briefings/cbp-8027/.
9. Industrial Strategy Council, 'UK Regional Productivity Differences: An Evidence Review', 4 February 2020: https://industrialstrategycouncil.org/uk-regional-productivity-differences-evidence-review.
10. Department for Levelling Up, Housing and Communities, 'Levelling Up the United Kingdom', 4 February 2020: https://www.gov.uk/government/publications/levelling-up-the-united-kingdom.

11. Ian Warren, 'Watch Out, Tories. Your Southern Strongholds Are Turning Red', *Guardian*, 9 May 2018: https://www.theguardian.com/commentisfree/2018/may/09/tories-southern-red-south-england-london.

12. Department for Work and Pensions, 'Households Below Average Income: 1994/95 to 2017/18', 28 March 2019: https://www.gov.uk/government/statistics/households-below-average-income-199495-to-201718.

13. Thomas Friedman, 'A Warning From the Garden', *New York Times*, 19 January 2007: https://www.nytimes.com/2007/01/19/opinion/19friedman.html.

14. Aditya Chakrabortty, 'Muddled, Top-Down, Technocratic: Why the Green New Deal Should be Scrapped', *Guardian*, 11 November 2021: https://www.theguardian.com/commentisfree/2021/nov/11/green-new-deal-bad-idea-policy-left-joe-biden-john-mcdonnell.

15. Terry Macalister, 'More Than Half of Jobs in UK Solar Industry Lost in Wake of Subsidy Cuts', *Guardian*, 11 June 2016: https://www.theguardian.com/environment/2016/jun/10/uk-solar-power-industry-job-losses-government-subsidy-cuts-energy-policy.

16. Charlotte Cox, 'Bus Drivers' Strike over 'Fire and Rehire' Could be on the Cusp of Breaking after 10-week Stalemate', *Manchester Evening News*, 6 May 2021: https://www.manchestereveningnews.co.uk/news/greater-manchester-news/go-north-west-strike-breaking-20531072.

17. Randeep Ramesh, 'Unite will Use "Brains as Well as Brawn" to Fight Bad Employers, Says Boss', *Guardian*, 2 December 2021: https://www.theguardian.com/politics/2021/dec/02/unite-will-use-brains-as-well-as-brawn-to-fight-bad-employers-says-boss?CMP=Share_iOSApp_Other.

18. 'Trade Union Membership, UK 1995–2021: Statistical Bulletin', 25 May 2022: https://assets.publishing.service.gov.uk/government/uploads/system/uploads/attachment_data/file/1077904/Trade_Union_Membership_UK_1995-2021_statistical_bulletin.pdf.

19. Anne-Marie Slaughter, 'Why Women Still Can't Have It All', *The Atlantic*, July/August 2021: https://www.theatlantic.com/magazine/archive/2012/07/why-women-still-cant-have-it-all/309020/?singlepage=true.

20. Criminal Justice System Delivery Data Dashboard, June 2022: https://criminal-justice-delivery-data-dashboards.justice.gov.uk/.

21. Rajeev Syal, 'Undercover Job Hunters Reveal Huge Race Bias in Britain's Workplaces', *Guardian*, 18 October 2009: https://www.theguardian.com/money/2009/oct/18/racism-discrimination-employment-undercover.

22. Jack Britton, Lorraine Dearden, Laura van der Erve and Ben Waltmann, 'The Impact of Undergraduate Degrees on Lifetime Earnings', Institute for Fiscal Studies, 29 February 2020: https://ifs.org.uk/publications/14729.

23. Nicola Woolcock, Rachel Sylvester and Emma Yeomans, 'Tony Blair Defends Target of Sending 50% to University', *The Times*, 7 June 2021: https://www.thetimes.co.uk/article/tony-blair-defends-target-of-sending-50-to-university-c363m0gzm.

24. Richard Adams, 'Poorest School-Leavers Half as Likely to Attend University as their Peers", *Guardian*, 14 December 2017: https://www.theguardian.com/education/2017/dec/14/poorest-school-leavers-half-as-likely-to-attend-university-as-their-peers.

25. From a forthcoming report by Ian Warren for Centre for Towns.

26. Michael Young, *The Rise of the Meritocracy*, London: Routledge, 1958.

27. Michael J. Sandel, *The Tyranny of Merit: What's Become of the Common Good?* London: Allen Lane, 2020.

28. Interview, Michael Sandel: 'The Populist Backlash has been a Revolt against the Tyranny of Merit', *Guardian*, 6 September 2020: https://www.theguardian.com/books/2020/sep/06/michael-sandel-the-populist-backlash-has-been-a-revolt-against-the-tyranny-of-merit.

29. Select Committee on Environment, Transport and Regional Affairs, 'First Report: Potential Risk of Fire Spread in Buildings via External Cladding Systems', n.d.: https://publications.parliament.uk/pa/cm199900/cmselect/cmenvtra/109/10907.htm.

30. Kenan Malik, 'Grenfell Delivers Yet More Horrors But the Guilty Still Fail to Take Responsibility', *Guardian*, 12 December 2021: https://www.theguardian.com/commentisfree/2021/dec/12/grenfell-delivers-yet-more-horrors-but-the-guilty-still-fail-to-take-responsibility.

31. Torsten Bell, 'In Britain, the Rich are Richer but the Poor Far Poorer than in Europe', *Guardian*, 25 April 2021: https://www.theguardian.com/commentisfree/2021/apr/25/in-britain-the-rich-are-richer-but-the-poor-far-poorer-than-in-europe#:~:text=Typical%20households%20in%20the%20UK,inequality%20many%20can%20live%20with.

32. The Equality Trust, 'The Scale of Economic Inequality in the UK', n.d.: https://equalitytrust.org.uk/scale-economic-inequality-uk.

33. Office for National Statistics, 'Household Total Wealth in Great Britain: April 2018 to March 2020', 7 January 2022: https://www.ons.gov.uk/peoplepopulationandcommunity/personaland householdfinances/incomeandwealth/bulletins/totalwealthin greatbritain/april2018tomarch2020.

34. BBC News, *Panorama*, 'Greensill: David Cameron "made $10m" before company's collapse', 9 August 2021: https://www.bbc.co.uk/news/uk-58149765.

35. C. Wright Mills, *The Power Elite*, Oxford: Oxford University Press, 1956.

36. Murad Ahmed and Andrew England, 'How a Saudi-Led Consortium Won Control of Newcastle United', *Financial Times*, 8 October 2021: https://www.ft.com/content/ed0d401a-ff9b-4199-9f5f-7a2a3e5727ca.

37. Annette Hastings, Nick Bailey, Glen Bramley, Maria Gannon and David Watkins, 'The Cost of the Cuts: The Impact on Local Government and Poorer Communities', Joseph Rowntree Foundation, March 2015: https://www.jrf.org.uk/sites/default/files/jrf/migrated/files/Summary-Final.pdf.

38. Philip McCann, 'Perceptions of Regional Inequality and the Geography of Discontent: Insights from the UK', *Regional Studies*, 54: 2 (2020): https://www.tandfonline.com/doi/full/10.1080/00343404.2019.1619928.

39. Maya Wolfe-Robinson, 'Most of UK's Levelling Up Taskforce Based in London, Figures Reveal', *Guardian*, 23 January 2022: https://www.theguardian.com/politics/2022/jan/23/most-of-uk-levelling-up-taskforce-based-in-london-figures-reveal.

40. National Infrastructure Commission: https://nic.org.uk/about/governance/.

41. Luke Raikes and Rosie Lockwood, 'Revealed: North Set to Receive £2,389 Less Per Person than London on Transport', IPPR, 19 August 2019: https://www.ippr.org/news-and-media/press-releases/revealed-north-set-to-receive-2-389-less-per-person-than-london-on-transport.

42. Ian Warren, 'Report: Our Towns Lag Behind on Foreign Direct Investment', Centre for Towns, 6 October 2019: https://www.centrefortowns.org/blog/37-report-our-towns-lag-behind-on-foreign-direct-investment.

43. https://assets.ey.com/content/dam/ey-sites/ey-com/en_uk/news/2023/6/uk-and-scotland-attractiveness-survey-2023.pdf

44. BBC News, 'Blair Joins Scottish Devolution Campaign Trail', n.d.: https://www.bbc.co.uk/news/special/politics97/news/09/0908/scotland.shtml.

45. David Williamson, 'A Storyteller who has Earned his Place in the Story of Wales: An Obituary for Rhodri Morgan', *Wales Online*, 18 May 2017: https://www.walesonline.co.uk/news/politics/storyteller-who-earned-place-story-13052371.

46. David Torrance, 'Devolution in Wales: 'A Process, not an Event", House of Commons Library, 4 May 2022: https://commonslibrary.parliament.uk/research-briefings/cbp-8318/.

47. Hansard, 6 January 2015, Column 135: https://publications. parliament.uk/pa/cm201415/cmhansrd/cm150106/debtext/ 150106-0001.htm.
48. 'Channel 4 News Boss Dorothy Byrne's MacTaggart Lecture in Full', *Press Gazette*, 22 August 2019: https://pressgazette.co.uk/ channel-4-news-boss-dorothy-byrnes-mactaggart-lecture-in-full/.
49. John F. Kennedy, *Profiles in Courage*, New York: Harpers, 1956.

5. THE ROAD TO POWER

1. 'Britain isn't Working', *New Statesman*, 2 September 2021: https:// www.newstatesman.com/economy/2021/09/leader-britain-isnt-working.
2. 'Address by Attorney General Robert F. Kennedy', Department of Justice, 20 May 1964: https://www.justice.gov/sites/default/files/ag/ legacy/2011/01/20/05-20-1964.pdf.
3. Nicholas Watt, 'David Cameron: Profit and Tax Cuts are not Dirty Words', *Guardian*, 2 October 2013: https://www.theguardian.com/ politics/2013/oct/02/david-cameron-conservative-conference-speech.
4. David Cameron, Speech, 'Making British Poverty History', 16 October 2007: https://conservative-speeches.sayit.mysociety.org/ speech/599767.
5. James Browne and Andrew Hood, 'Living Standards, Poverty and Inequality in the UK: 2015–16 to 2020–21', Institute for Fiscal Studies, February 2016: https://ifs.org.uk/uploads/publications/ comms/R114.pdf.
6. Michael Walzer, *Spheres of Justice*, New York: Basic Books, 1983.
7. Nick Timothy, 'Capitalism as we know it has failed. Not even the Tories can defend it', *The Telegraph*, 2 July 2023, https://www. telegraph.co.uk/news/2023/07/02/capitalism-has-failed-even-the-tories-cant-defend-it/
8. Matthew Keep, 'Country and Regional Public Sector Finances'.
9. Industrial Strategy Council, 'UK Regional Productivity Differences: An Evidence Review'.
10. GMCA, 'Greater Manchester Independent Prosperity Review', March 2019: https://www.greatermanchester-ca.gov.uk/what-we-do/economy/greater-manchester-independent-prosperity-review/.
11. 'Levelling Up the United Kingdom', Department for Levelling Up, Housing and Communities, 2 February 2022: https://www.gov.uk/ government/publications/levelling-up-the-united-kingdom.
12. Warren, 'Watch out, Tories. Your Southern Strongholds are Turning Red'; Department for Work and Pensions, 'Households Below Average Income: 1994/95 to 2017/18'.

13. Julian Coman, 'Can Labour Think Big and Make Levelling Up Work?', *Observer*, 24 July 2022: https://www.theguardian.com/inequality/2022/jul/24/can-labour-think-big-and-make-levelling-up-work.

14. Norman, *The Big Society: The Anatomy of the New Politics*.

15. Tracy Crouch, 'Fan-Led Review of Football Governance: Securing the Game's Future', Department for Digital, Media, Culture & Sport, 24 November 2021: https://www.gov.uk/government/publications/fan-led-review-of-football-governance-securing-the-games-future/fan-led-review-of-football-governance-securing-the-games-future.

16. Damian Carrington, 'UK Cancels Pioneering £1bn Carbon Capture and Storage Competition', *Guardian*, 25 November 2015: https://www.theguardian.com/environment/2015/nov/25/uk-cancels-pioneering-1bn-carbon-capture-and-storage-competition.

17. Tom Archer, Elaine Batty, Cathy Harris, Stephen Parks, Ian Wilson, Mike Aiken, Eliza Buckley, Rebecca Moran and Vita Terry, 'Our Assets, Our Future: The Economics, Outcomes and Sustainability of Assets in Community Ownership', Power to Change, July 2019: https://www.powertochange.org.uk/wp-content/uploads/2019/07/Assets-Report-DIGITAL-1.pdf.

18. Patrick Collinson and Rupert Jones, 'Wonga Collapses into Administration', *Guardian*, 30 August 2018: https://www.theguardian.com/business/2018/aug/30/wonga-collapses-into-administration.

19. Rachel Reeves, *The Everyday Economy*, 2018: https://www.rachelreevesmp.co.uk/wp-content/uploads/sites/96/2020/09/374425087-Rachel-Reeves-The-Everyday-Economy-1.pdf.

20. Tim Leunig and James Swaffield, Edited by Oliver Marc Hartwich, 'Cities Unlimited: Making Urban Regeneration Work', Policy Exchange, 2007: https://www.policyexchange.org.uk/wp-content/uploads/2016/09/cities-unlimited-aug-08.pdf.

21. Rachel Wearmouth, 'Top Rishi Sunak Aide Said Workers in Northern Towns Should "Accept Lower Wages", *Mirror*, 8 February 2022: https://www.mirror.co.uk/news/politics/top-rishi-sunak-aide-said-26161330.

22. Andrew Baker, Gerald Epstein and Juan Montecino, 'The UK's Finance Curse? Costs and Processes', Sheffield Political Economy Research Institute, September 2018: http://speri.dept.shef.ac.uk/wp-content/uploads/2019/01/SPERI-The-UKs-Finance-Curse-Costs-and-Processes.pdf.

23. Alfie Stirling and Loren King, 'Financing Investment Reforming Finance Markets for the Long Term', IPPR Commission on Economic Justice, July 2017: www.ippr.org/files/2017-07/cejfinance-and-investment-discussion-paper-a4-report-17-07-21.pdf.

24. 'UK Bank Branch Numbers Have Almost Halved Since 2015, Analysis Finds', *Guardian*, 27 December 2021: https://www. theguardian.com/business/2021/dec/27/uk-bank-branch-numbers-have-almost-halved-since-2015.

25. 'Exclusive: hundreds of "ATM deserts" identified in the UK', *Which?*, 14 November 2019: https://www.which.co.uk/ news/2019/11/exclusive-hundreds-of-atm-deserts-identified-in-the-uk/.

26. Press Release, 'Economy Minister Sets out Plans for Banc Cambria, Wales' New Community Bank', 14 December 2021: https://gov. wales/economy-minister-sets-out-plans-banc-cambria-wales-new-community-bank.

27. 'Community Banking', Middleton Cooperating, n.d.: https:// middleton.coop/node/28.

28. Industrial Strategy Commission, 'The Final Report of the Industrial Strategy Commission', November 2017: https://drive. google.com/file/d/1TiOMDGya6BSrmQvauGBc0tHHo5nfiHRG/ view.

29. Bobby Kennedy, University of Kansas, 18 March 1968.

30. UNICEF, 'Child Poverty in Perspective: An Overview of Child Well-Being in Rich Countries', 2007: https://www.unicef-irc.org/ publications/pdf/rc7_eng.pdf.

31. Philip McCann, 'Space-Blind and Place-Based Policy: Initiatives for Fostering Innovation and Growth', Sheffield University Management School, November 2021: https://gold.uclg.org/sites/ default/files/gold_vi_working_paper_04.pdf.

32. Philip McCann, 'Space-Blind and Place-Based Policy'.

33. Industrial Strategy Commission, 'The Final Report of the Industrial Strategy Commission'.

34. Bennett Institute for Public Policy, 'Policies for Places as Well as People', 6 July 2022: https://www.bennettinstitute.cam.ac.uk/blog/ policies-for-places-as-well-as-people/.

35. Raikes and Lockwood, 'Revealed: North Set to Receive £2,389 Less Per Person than London on Transport'.

36. James Reid, 'Alienation', University of Glasgow, 28 April 1973: https://www.gla.ac.uk/media/Media_167194_smxx.pdf.

6. OF THE PEOPLE, FOR THE PEOPLE, BY THE PEOPLE, WITH THE PEOPLE

1. Jennifer Williams, 'Andy Burnham's Warning Over a "Swiss-Cheese" NHS with Cities Opting Out', *Manchester Evening News*, 28 February 2015: https://www.manchestereveningnews.co. uk/news/health/andy-burnhams-warning-over-swiss-cheese-8721228.

ENDNOTES

2. Lisa Nandy, 'Real Devolution has to Come from Public Consent, not Whitehall Diktat', *New Statesman*, 27 February 2015: https://www.newstatesman.com/politics/2015/02/real-devolution-has-come-public-consent-not-whitehall-diktat.

3. Department for Levelling Up, Housing and Communities, 'Levelling Up the United Kingdom'.

4. Local Government Association, 'Delivering Local Net Zero', 17 October 2021: https://www.local.gov.uk/publications/delivering-local-net-zero.

5. Andy Street, 'Devolved Regional Powers are Chance to Make a Difference to Net Zero', *The Times*, 13 July 2021: https://www.thetimes.co.uk/article/devolved-regional-powers-are-chance-to-make-a-difference-to-net-zero-crt26lnf8.

6. House of Commons Housing, Communities and Local Government Committee, 'Progress on devolution in England', 1 October 2021: https://committees.parliament.uk/publications/7467/documents/78200/default/.

7. Beth Abbit, 'The "World-Famous Burnley Market": Rishi Sunak Confuses Burnley and Bury During Awkward BBC Interview', *Manchester Evening News*, 28 October 2021: https://www.manchestereveningnews.co.uk/news/greater-manchester-news/world-famous-burnley-market-rishi-21992171.

8. Hélène Mulholland, 'North-East Voters Reject Regional Assembly', *Guardian*, 5 November 2004: https://www.theguardian.com/society/2004/nov/05/regionalgovernment.politics.

9. For example House of Commons Housing, Communities and Local Government Committee, 'Progress on devolution in England'; The Devolution All-Party Parliamentary Group, 'Levelling-up Devo: The Role of National Government in Making a Success of Devolution in England', n.d.: https://connectpa.co.uk/devolution-appg/levelling-up-devo/.

10. Citizens' Assembly, 'Revitalising Democracy in South Yorkshire: The Report of Assembly North', January 2016: https://citizensassembly.co.uk/assembly-north-overview-report/#Executive-Summary.

11. Housing, Communities and Local Government Committee, 'Oral Evidence: Progress on Devolution in England, HC 174', 22 June 2020: https://committees.parliament.uk/oralevidence/555/html/.

12. Housing, Communities and Local Government Committee, 'Oral Evidence: Progress on Devolution in England, HC 174'.

13. Jennifer Williams, 'Is Greater Manchester Politically Accountable Enough for a £1bn "Levelling Up" Deal?', *Manchester Evening News*, 7 October 2021: https://www.manchestereveningnews.co.uk/news/greater-manchester-news/greater-manchester-politically-accountable-enough-21797823.

14. House of Commons Housing, Communities and Local Government Committee, 'Progress on Devolution in England'.
15. Parliament UK, 'Party Politics and Organisational Culture', 14 December 2017, https://publications.parliament.uk/pa/cm201719/cmselect/cmcomloc/369/36906.htm.
16. Communities and Local Government, 'Communities in the Driving Seat: A Study of Participatory Budgeting in England: Final Report, August 2011: https://assets.publishing.service.gov.uk/government/uploads/system/uploads/attachment_data/file/6152/19932231.pdf.
17. The King's Fund, 'A Citizen-Led Approach to Health and Care: Lessons from the Wigan Deal', 26 June 2019: https://www.kingsfund.org.uk/publications/wigan-deal.
18. Raphaël Besson, 'How Madrid's Residents are Using Open-Source Urban Planning to Create Shared Spaces – and Build Democracy', The Conversation, 27 June 2017: https://theconversation.com/how-madrids-residents-are-using-open-source-urban-planning-to-create-shared-spaces-and-build-democracy-79717.
19. House of Commons library, 'Supported Exempt Accommodation (England)', 30 June 2022: https://commonslibrary.parliament.uk/research-briefings/cbp-9362/#:~:text=Data%20gathered%20by%20Crisis%2C%20the,a%2062%25%20increase%20since%202016.
20. Guy Shrubsole, Who Owns England? How We Lost Our Land and How to Take It Back, London: HarperCollins, 2019.
21. Centre for Public Data, 'New Data on Property in England & Wales Owned by Overseas Individuals', 12 November 2021: https://www.centreforpublicdata.org/property-data-overseas-individuals.
22. Jack Shenker, 'Revealed: The Insidious Creep of Pseudo-Public Space in London', Guardian, 24 July 2017: https://www.theguardian.com/cities/2017/jul/24/revealed-pseudo-public-space-pops-london-investigation-map.
23. Meg Russell, 'Representing the Nations and Regions in a New Upper House: Lessons from Overseas', The Constitution Unit, University College London, n.d.: https://www.ucl.ac.uk/constitution-unit/sites/constitution-unit/files/50.pdf.
24. Media Reform Coalition, 'Who Owns the Uk Media?', March 2019: https://www.mediareform.org.uk/wp-content/uploads/2019/03/FINALonline2.pdf.
25. Dominic Ponsford, 'Four Men Own Britain's News Media. Is That a Problem for Democracy?', New Statesman, 16 February 2021: https://www.newstatesman.com/business/2021/02/four-men-own-britain-s-news-media-problem-democracy.
26. 'The Cairncross Review: A Sustainable Future for Journalism', 12 February 2019: https://assets.publishing.service.gov.uk/

government/uploads/system/uploads/attachment_data/
file/779882/021919_DCMS_Cairncross_Review_.pdf.

27. 'Written Evidence Submitted by BBC World Service', September 2020: https://committees.parliament.uk/writtenevidence/10939/html/.

28. Anthony Blinken, Speech: https://www.nytimes.com/2021/03/03/us/politics/biden-blinken-foreign-policy.html#:~:text=%E2%80%9CI%20know%20that%20foreign%20policy,or%20it%20fades%20from%20view.%E2%80%9D.

29. 'Churchill's Three Circles', n.d.: https://web-archives.univ-pau.fr/english/special/SRdoc1.pdf.

30. Catherine Belton, *Putin's People*, Glasgow: William Collins, 2020.

31. https://www.ft.com/content/59f9d0a6-229f-4b70-99be-9df4be202b99.

32. Amnesty International, 'Trafigura: A Toxic Journey, n.d.: https://www.amnesty.org/en/latest/news/2016/04/trafigura-a-toxic-journey/.

33. Sophia Gaston, 'Annual Survey of UK Public Opinion on Foreign Policy and Global Britain', 15 June 2022: https://bfpg.co.uk/2022/06/2022-annual-survey/.

34. 'The Great Benefits Row: Channel 4 Dispatches', 11 April 2016: https://www.channel4.com/press/news/great-benefits-row-channel-4-dispatches.

35. Chaminda Jayanetti, 'UK Government's £2.9bn job Search Scheme has Put Only 7% of Participants in Work to Date', 5 June 2022: https://www.theguardian.com/society/2022/jun/05/uk-governments-restart-scheme-fails-to-find-work-for-93-per-cent-of-people?amp.

36. Rowena Mason, 'Charities Should Stick to Knitting and Keep Out of Politics, says MP', 3 September 2013: https://www.theguardian.com/society/2014/sep/03/charities-knitting-politics-brooknewmark.

37. Sandra Laville, 'UK Charities Call for End to "Gagging Law" in Run-Up to Elections', 20 November 2019: https://www.theguardian.com/society/2019/nov/20/charities-call-for-end-gagging-law-lobbying-act-run-up-elections.

38. Michael Walzer, 'The Historical Task of the Left in the Present Period', *Dissent*, 2 January 2017: https://www.dissentmagazine.org/online_articles/historical-task-of-left-present-period-trump.

39. Caritas Anchor House, 'The Cardinal Manning Catholic Social Teaching Conference 2014', 19 June 2014: https://www.caritasanchorhouse.org.uk/sites/default/files/wp-content/uploads/2014/08/CM-Report1.pdf.

40. Isabel Hardman, *Why We Get the Wrong Politicians*, London: Atlantic Books, 2018.

41. Jess Phillips, '*Why We Get the Wrong Politicians* is a Vital and Compelling Read', 5 September 2018, updated 25 July 2021: https://www.newstatesman.com/culture/2018/09/why-we-get-wrong-politicians-vital-and-compelling-read.

42. Archie Brown, *The Myth of the Strong Leader*, London: Bodley Head, 2014.

43. Jeremy Armstrong, 'Beijing Olympics: Opening ceremony star mimed because real singer judged not pretty enough', 13 August 2008, updated 28 January 2012: https://www.mirror.co.uk/news/uk-news/beijing-olympics-opening-ceremony-star-326908.

44. 'London 2012: Opening Ceremony – Reviews', 29 July 2012: https://www.theguardian.com/sport/2012/jul/29/london-2012-opening-ceremony-reviews.

7. THE TILT

1. Maria Sobolewska and Rob Ford, *Brexitland: Identity, Diversity and the Reshaping of British Politics*, Cambridge: Cambridge University Press, 2020.

2. Sobolewska and Ford, *Brexitland*.